Pi

LIFE WITH ____ ___

"One need not take ghosts literally in order to benefit from the lessons Bruni's learned serving both the haunted and the haunting."

—*New York Times*

"You don't get more legit than Amy when it comes to ghost hunting and investigating the paranormal. Her pragmatic approach to a subject matter that is often full of hysteria is so refreshing and real. If you want to read a book about how things really are when it comes to ghost hunting…this is it."

—Jack Osbourne

"A field guide to things that go bump in the night. Amy's boundless curiosity for the unknown shines through like a bright flashlight in the darkest night."

—Josh Gates, host, *Expedition Unknown*

"Amy Bruni is one of the world's preeminent paranormal investigators. In her first book, Amy shares her vast knowledge about ghosts and her experience in dealing with the afterlife. Take it from me: Spirits are giving this book two tremendous thumbs up."

—Chip Coffey, psychic, medium, and TV personality

"Full of astonishing and deeply moving stories... Extraordinary, insightful, thought provoking, inherently fascinating, and very highly recommended reading."

—Midwest Book Review

"Bruni's conversational style and ghost-hunting tips that also serve as life tips (go in with an open mind, don't judge, beware of your own bias), plus the fact that she makes no attempt to win over non-believers, make this a perfect read for fans and anyone interested in the paranormal."

—Booklist

"If you're into real-life(?) ghost stories and the people who investigate them, here's a read for you."

—Book Riot

LIFE
WITH THE
AFTERLIFE

13 Truths I Learned about Ghosts

AMY BRUNI
with Julie Tremaine

GRAND CENTRAL
PUBLISHING

NEW YORK   BOSTON

Grand Central Publishing
Hachette Book Group
1290 Avenue of the Americas, New York, NY 10104
grandcentralpublishing.com
twitter.com/grandcentralpub

First published in hardcover and ebook October 2020
First Trade Paperback Edition: October 2022

Grand Central Publishing is a division of Hachette Book Group, Inc. The Grand Central Publishing name and logo is a trademark of Hachette Book Group, Inc.

The publisher is not responsible for websites (or their content) that are not owned by the publisher.

The Hachette Speakers Bureau provides a wide range of authors for speaking events. To find out more, go to www.hachettespeakersbureau.com or call (866) 376-6591.

LCCN: 9781538754146

ISBNs: 978-1-5387-5412-2 (trade paperback), 978-1-5387-5413-9 (ebook)

Printed in Canada

FRI-C

10 9 8 7 6 5 4 3 2 1

For Charlotte
Nothing makes me happier than raising you
in my magical, ghostly world. I love you and
I can't wait to read your book one day.

And for Mom
I miss you constantly. I can say with
certainty you're the ghost I wish I'd find
more than any other.

Contents

Introduction

WELCOME TO THE STRANGE SIDE

If you had told me one day there would be a drinking game devoted to every time I got a swear word bleeped out on television, I would have told you that you were f***ing crazy. And yet, here we are.

You might recognize me from *Kindred Spirits*, or from *Ghost Hunters*, or from lots of weird and fun paranormal events all over the country. But what you probably don't realize is that I know a lot less about the afterlife than I did when I began investigating and researching unexplained phenomena. I started out with a very distinct idea of what I believed, and what I thought ghosts and spirits were. The more I learned, the more I realized I have no idea.

So when I say this book is "thirteen truths" about the

afterlife, what I really mean is these are thirteen different ways of learning about ghosts and the paranormal, of opening your mind to new possibilities, of challenging your expectations, and of considering other perspectives and new ideas. The very nature of paranormal investigation prevents us from having any answers to the questions we are raising. No scientific tests exist to prove these paranormal phenomena we experience are real; there are no definitive conclusions to reach. There are only new experiences, and new ways of thinking.

People who have been seriously doing this work are the first ones to tell you they can't say for sure what the paranormal is, and they will never pretend to have any solid answers. I hope you didn't come to this book looking for me to explain the unexplainable. This book is a conversation between me and my ideas, you and your ideas, and the perspectives of many other experts in the field who have spent years and years developing their own theories.

This book, too, owes a debt to all the weird and wonderful paranormal researchers whom I've worked with throughout my career. Ghost hunting doesn't happen in a vacuum. It's working with other people who are equally as passionate about discovering the unknown corners of existence as I am that has truly allowed me to grow as an investigator, and to develop the theories and practices that have led me to where I am today. My hope is you'll read this, stretch the boundaries of what you think is possible, and reach outside the box the next time you are trying to rationalize something that defies explanation. And, you know, get a little bit scared in the process, because that's half the fun.

Thank you for coming on this journey with me. Now let's get strange.

LIFE

WITH THE

AFTERLIFE

Chapter 1

GHOSTS ARE PEOPLE, TOO

FOR WALT DISNEY, it all started with a mouse. But for me, it all started with a ghost.

When I was growing up, it was just an accepted part of life that our house in Alameda, California, was haunted. From the moment we moved into our little Craftsman bungalow, it was clear there were ghosts in the house, and my New Agey parents certainly didn't shy away from that idea. In fact, they encouraged me, my brother, and my two sisters *not* to be afraid of what we couldn't explain. We felt spirits in the house, and we talked about them. My mom, especially, talked about seeing a little boy running between rooms. My dad dabbled in supernatural research. To us, it didn't feel weird at all. *Sometimes there are ghosts,* the thinking was in our family, *and sometimes they're in our house*. It was totally normal to us.

Totally normal, right?

Maybe it sounds strange now, but that thinking opened a whole world to me. I was raised to be receptive to the idea that there are things in the universe we can't easily understand, and I was never told I should be wary of them. This paved a path of weird and wonderful possibilities I never could have imagined as a carefree child of the eighties, playing outside until after dark every night in Northern California.

So the night I saw a man standing in the window, eight feet above the ground, in a place where there was nowhere to stand, and wearing a kind of clothing I had never seen before, I knew I was seeing a ghost. But I wasn't scared.

Since then, there have been many moments in my career as a paranormal investigator when I have been frightened. Sometimes, downright terrified. But not at that moment. At that moment, I saw a man who couldn't possibly be there. He wasn't a scary ghost to me. He was a person.

So I did what any normal kid would do. I ran to get my mom.

By the time we got back, he was gone. It had just been a flash, for only a moment. But I knew what I'd seen. The man was wearing an old-fashioned green uniform and standing in the window, in clear view, even though that window was eight feet off the ground.

Alameda, a midsize city in the San Francisco Bay Area, has a long military history. Even now, after the base has closed, it's still home to the Naval Air Museum. We learned later that our little house had been military housing, and a family who'd lived there had had a son who died serving in World War II. There used to be a wraparound porch where I had seen him standing, which explains why he was visible in a window so high off the ground. When he lived there, he would have been standing on that porch.

A man who wasn't there, standing on a porch that wasn't there.

You might say my whole life has been a path leading me to professional ghost hunting.

After that day, my appetite for weird knowledge was insatiable: about the afterlife, about who that ghost might be, about anything pertaining to the supernatural and anything not easily explained. My mom, Debbie, would drop me off at the library, and I would head straight for the ghost section. I read everything I could get my hands on by Hans Holzer, the famed paranormal researcher who investigated the house from *The Amityville Horror.* I examined and reexamined old photos of mediums in ridiculous situations, like having ectoplasm coming out of their ears. In the eighties there was a huge interest in the unexplained and there were new books coming out faster than I could keep up with them. (Holzer himself wrote more than 120.) I devoured as much as I could, and I accepted it all as fact. Now I have a better understanding of how to determine what is credible when it comes to evidence. Back then, it never occurred to me that any of it was fake, and I loved every word of what I was reading.

At home, spooky things kept happening. The ghost of a little boy showed up more and more. Once, our neighbors were over for dinner. They had a young son who was about my age, who had fallen asleep on the couch at some point in the evening. His mom kept looking toward the bathroom. "Where's Alex?" she asked. "I saw him go in there and I thought he'd be out by now."

"Alex is asleep on the couch, sweetie," her husband replied.

Her face went white. She was sure she had seen her son get up and walk across the room. Positive. But it wasn't her son she was seeing. It was the boy who had passed away from leukemia years and years ago. At another dinner with that same couple, my dad, Gene, told them about the ghost, and how he would appear often in the house. They were totally skeptical, saying they didn't believe in ghosts or the supernatural, and that none of it was possible. They said this even though we all knew they had seen the same paranormal activity we had. And then a picture came off the wall, hovered in midair for a moment or two, and crashed to the ground.

They left and never came back. The woman would

come into our yard, but neither she nor her husband ever set foot in our house again.

I know now that there are many instances when paranormal activity ramps up in a location once people start acknowledging the presence of ghosts, especially in homes with lots of kids, like ours. They know we can see them, or hear them, and they want to make contact, so they try even harder to get our attention. The idea that we could talk to them, or ask them what they wanted to say, wasn't a theory I had back then. We were just wondering what was going to happen next.

When I was maybe eight years old, I took a picture of my sister standing on the porch of our house. I thought she was the only person I was photographing. When the film was developed, though, we all saw an image of an elderly woman standing behind her. My mom took it to our photographer neighbor to ask if it was a double exposure or something similar. The neighbor replied that it looked to her like the elderly woman who had lived in the house before we did. Evidently, when her husband would leave, she would stand in that spot and wait for him to come home.

Was it a spirit photo? I can't say for sure. It definitely looked that way to me, but whether it was or not, it sparked something in my mind. *There are actually people who look for ghosts*, I realized. *I could look for them, too.*

I didn't think about it that way at the time, but knowing

the stories of the people who lived in our house before we did, and who stayed with us in the house after they died, formed a different perspective about ghost hunting in me. Like many people, I started investigating the paranormal as a hobby. All those hours in the library poring over books eventually turned into a desire to find more ghosts in real life. But for me, it was always important to have a knowledge base—who I might find, why that soul is still there, what this spirit needs to hear or experience to feel like they can move on.

My dad, seeing an opportunity for both quality time together and for teachable moments, started taking me on paranormal investigations to supposedly haunted locations. We went to places like Fort Ross, the site of a Russian settlement from the early 1800s where the oldest known graves in Sonoma County are located. When I was in high school, he would pique my interest in historic locations in California by telling me there were ghosts there. We'd go with an old tape recorder, a Polaroid camera, and a notebook filled with research notes—a far cry from the ghost hunting equipment we use on the show now—and just sit there, asking questions, using what we knew about the place to inform our EVP sessions. (EVP is short for "electronic voice phenomena," and it's what a recorder will pick up that we can't hear with our own ears. We'll talk a lot more about this later.)

I'd spent so much time learning about the paranormal

that it was a total rush to put it all into practice. Suddenly, I was doing it myself: using all the things I had heard about research and investigating to try to make contact with the other side. But it wasn't about trying to be scared—or, at least, not *only* wanting to be scared. It was about learning who these ghosts were in life and why they were still around now. I was trying to figure out why they were making contact with the living. For my dad, it was about spending time together and simultaneously teaching me about history. It was incredibly effective and so interesting. Those times we had together are some of my best childhood memories. Using haunted history to teach kids about the past is something I tell other parents about all the time, and something I definitely plan on putting into practice if my daughter Charlotte grows up to have an interest in ghosts.

Eventually, I started taking vacations to do amateur investigations at haunted locations like the Stanley Hotel in Colorado, from *The Shining*, and the *Queen Mary*, a notoriously haunted cruise ship that's now a hotel permanently docked in Los Angeles. It was definitely a thrill to put all my preparation into action, and in the beginning, I really was scared and felt the adrenaline rush of brushes with the unexplained.

Through those investigations, through finding the people behind the scares, I eventually realized something so simple, but so often overlooked by enthusiasts of the paranormal: *Ghosts are people, too.* As much as ghost hunting is about the excitement of making contact, it's also about something else. You're talking to a person on the other side. A person who was once alive, and a person who is in a position that you could potentially end up in yourself one day.

They're not sticking around for the hell of it—okay, maybe that's a bad choice of words—but they're certainly not sticking around for the fun of it. (Seriously, does haunting the same three rooms for two hundred years sound like fun to you?) My theory, like many people's, is that usually they're still here because they have unfinished business on this plane. Sometimes, it's because they have things they want to communicate. Sometimes, they don't even know they've passed away and that it's time to go.

Those restless spirits want to be heard. They *need* to be heard. And those of us who are lucky enough to get to talk to them have a responsibility to listen, really listen, and not just try to treat them like an evening's entertainment. There were so many times on *Ghost Hunters* when my investigating partner Adam Berry and I would find ghosts who were so clearly in need of help—but because of filming constraints and the format of the show, we'd have to leave before we could do much to aid them. That show was designed around helping people figure out whether they had hauntings in their homes and businesses, not to help the dead with whatever was keeping them on this plane. The more often this happened, the guiltier we felt.

We once filmed an episode of *Ghost Hunters* at the Waverly Hills Sanatorium in Kentucky, which is an enormous hospital that once held up to four hundred patients at a time at the height of the tuberculosis epidemic in the early twentieth century. After the TB hospital was closed, Waverly Hills became a long-term care facility for the elderly and mentally ill, which was finally shuttered due to claims of patient neglect. Current owner Tina Mattingly, who purchased the building long afterward, claims that anywhere from 20,000 to 62,000 people have died there in the 120 years Waverly Hills has been around.

During filming, Adam and I were in the nurses' wing, which had never been professionally investigated before. For all we knew, we were the first people in that area in decades. At the end of the night, at maybe 2 a.m., we started communicating through a series of knocks with some ghosts we thought were nurses. We made the communication choices clear: Knock once for yes, and twice for no. It was constant—they were answering every question, and their responses were clear and consistent.

At one point, we asked them, "How many of you are there here? Knock wherever you are in the room." We heard knocks all around us. Seventeen of them, as though there were seventeen different people trying to reach out to us.

We asked, "Do you want prayer?" *One knock.* So we prayed for them. I wouldn't call myself a really religious person, but if someone is asking me to pray for them, I'm going to. I believe it's all about energy and intention. As we prayed, it was completely silent all around us. No knocking at all. But as soon as we said "Amen," the knocks started back up again. It was almost as if they were trying to thank us.

The knocks kept happening. It seemed like the nurses were so eager to talk, to have someone acknowledge that they were actually there. We finally had to leave for the night, because the camera crew has limits on how long they can work in a day. We felt so bad when we told them we had to go. They clearly didn't want us to. As we were walking down the hallway, they knocked on the walls all around us, following us as we left the building.

I was in tears as we were leaving. It was heartbreaking to make contact with ghosts who so desperately wanted to communicate with us. I wanted to hear them, and try to help them, so badly. When I got back to my hotel room, as the sun was coming up, I heard one final knock on the wall above my bed.

Adam and I had a lot of experiences like this, where we saw a real need for help. There were spirits wanting to communicate messages to the living, or needing to fix a problem tethering them to a location, and yet, we couldn't resolve things for them. There were many times when we'd hear something say *Help me*, but we had to walk away because of the kind of show we were on and the constraints of that format. At the time, the common thinking was more about trying to find evidence that ghosts exist, and less about who those ghosts were and what they were saying. That was the public appetite when *Ghost Hunters* started: People wanted to know what we were finding, and whether it was real. So in the analysis at the end of an episode, we'd present these clear EVPs of people crying, or asking for help, but then no one would try to find out what they were asking for help with.

This is how the idea for *Kindred Spirits* materialized: from finding spirits in need and then having to leave them, knowing there was more work to do. It just felt like there was something *missing* from the conversation about ghosts. Eventually, Adam and I decided we needed to leave *Ghost Hunters* and find a way to bridge the gap between the living and the dead that addressed the needs of both sides like real people. We wanted to focus on what we could do to help all of them at the same time, and not just find evidence and leave. Ghosts aren't just for fun to me. They're people who have needs just like we do.

Now, through *Kindred Spirits*, we travel the country looking for people who really need our help. We have gone into the home of a woman who wasn't using an entire floor of her house because she believed it was haunted by her brother, who had been murdered by their other brother. We have investigated for a terrified mother and son who weren't using their living space because the son kept seeing a "shadow man." We've gone deep into the woods to try to figure out who was breaking things and scratching people at a family's cabin.

To help us get to the bottom of what's really going on, we often bring in local historians or other paranormal researchers. Chip Coffey is a psychic who once had his own show, *Psychic Kids*, and has joined us on many *Kindred Spirits* cases to try to get readings from spirits in the locations we're investigating.

"It's almost like social work for the living and the dead," Chip said. "It's attending to the needs of both. When we go in, we're trying to determine: What are the living experiencing there? And what are the dead experiencing?"

Do we really help? I'd like to think so. We dig deep into the history of the area, especially the history of the home, to try to find out what could be causing activity. We talk to family members of former residents, and family members of the people experiencing the activity. We've found gravestones hidden in backyards and wells in the basements of three-hundred-year-old homes. Creepy? Absolutely. But in all of those instances, even if a spirit has clearly just said that it wants to be left alone, I've walked away feeling like I did something to help someone, whether that person is alive or dead.

"A lot of times, I think they're just ready to have their full story told, or they're looking for someone who will actually listen to them, or pay them some attention, or get their story right," Chip explained. "It's like we're asking them what we can do to make their existence better.

"It's dealing with bringing some understanding, and hopefully comfort, to the people in the location who are still living, and addressing the needs of the dead," Chip continued. When it comes to talking to spirits, "I think the word is 'acknowledgment.' Maybe they're imparting information that no one has ever acknowledged from them, or a message they haven't been able to get across."

If there's one thing I hope you'll take away from this book, it's that most ghosts are not frightening. They are not some novelty sideshow act, either. We're all going to end up the same way in the end, and some of us are probably going to stay behind to finish what we couldn't in life. Most living people, though, see ghosts as scary. My feeling is that once we learn more about the spirit world, and the people who populate it, we start to humanize ghosts and become less afraid of them. That is exactly what happened to me, and it taught me to handle the paranormal with more respect. It has also brought me down the most unconventional career path I can think of, and taken me into some totally hair-raising situations. I have found myself everywhere from abandoned sanatoriums, to haunted prisons, to shuttered mental hospitals where spirits are, quite literally, coming out of the walls.

So for now, let's talk about some crazy good ghost stories.

BABY AMY AND BABY GHOSTS

When I was very young, maybe three or four, we lived in an apartment building. None of my siblings had been born yet, so it was just my mom, my dad, and me.

One day, I was playing in the living room and something caught my eye from my room. It was a shadow, peeking out of my bedroom closet. A very distinct little shadow figure, maybe the size of a kid like me, that definitely wanted to play.

It would peek its head out of the closet, then dart back in again, over and over like it was playing a game. Finally, my curiosity got the better of me, and I decided to go investigate. (You're shocked. I know.)

By the time I walked over, it had disappeared.

I remember that I wasn't scared, but more puzzled that something that had just been there was now gone.

Later, I asked my mom about it. She looked shocked for a moment, then glossed over it. It's the exact same thing I would do now if Charlotte saw a ghost and told me about it. Maybe it's genetic?

Chapter 2

GHOSTS AREN'T TRYING TO SCARE YOU

IT SOUNDS CRAZY, right? Walking into a place you suspect is haunted—if you don't have a lot of experience with it—is one of the scariest things you can do. Hell, sometimes it still scares me and I've done thousands of investigations at this point. But it really is true. You might feel afraid of what you see and experience (or even what you sense) in a place, but in almost every instance, the ghosts there aren't trying to frighten you. They are people trying to communicate the best way they know how, using the limited resources they have.

Over the years, I've seen so many instances of spirits who *seem* scary, who are really just having trouble being heard, and trying their hardest to get through. On Season

1 of *Kindred Spirits*, we visited a house in Connecticut that had real signs of a menacing presence. The homeowners were seeing looming shadow figures, hearing stomping sounds from the attic, and witnessing things thrown across rooms with no explanation. They felt as though their five-year-old son was being targeted. They had just bought the home and were terrified of what they might have gotten themselves into.

When Adam and I went to investigate, we couldn't get much through EVP sessions, so we started going through a list of the home's previous owners and asking if we were speaking to them. The only thing we got was one word: "Ko-tek." It turns out he was an early owner of the home, who emigrated from Poland and came to America through Ellis Island, but who never learned to speak English. When we brought in a translator, we could finally have a conversation with Mr. Kotek. Because he didn't speak the same language as the homeowners, he didn't understand that the mess and disarray in the home were from the new owners' renovations. Once he realized what was happening to what he still considered his home, and once it was explained to him in a language he could understand, the spirit of Mr. Kotek no longer came off as gruff and mean. The new owners were taking the kind of care of his house that he had taken himself, and he quieted down.

Sometimes, though, they *are* actually trying to scare

you, just for a laugh. That happened in the Randolph County Asylum/Infirmary in Winchester, Indiana, which we investigated in Season 4 of *Kindred.* It turned out the entity growling on the other side of a locked door, shaking it nearly off its hinges, was a carnival worker and sometimes-patient of the hospital named Harry "Peg" Dunn, a good-natured spirit who was just trying to have some fun and spice up an otherwise quiet afterlife. But that's another story.

I fully subscribe to the idea that people act in the afterlife the same way they acted in life. If someone was a jerk when he was alive, he's not necessarily going to *stop* being a jerk as a ghost. But to me, that's the vast minority of people. It's also possible that a person could be doing things that come off as scary, like Mr. Kotek, because that person doesn't understand what's happening in his home, or doesn't like what you're doing there. I genuinely feel Mr. Kotek was trying to protect his home from what he thought was a threat. More often than not, I think we perceive things we don't understand as scary because it's human nature to fear the unknown. It's easy to assume that a strange noise in your house has bad intent behind it. Unless you were raised in a totally weird home like I was, it's only natural to have that reaction. Me, I'm like, *Let's go find out what that was.*

People ask me all the time how I can hunt ghosts for a living—by which they mean, *How the hell are you putting yourself in these spine-chilling situations all the time? Are you insane?* What I tell them is exactly the opposite of what they're expecting to hear. I don't find ghosts scary. I find them fascinating. They're people with stories to tell, and I want to hear them. To me, investigating a haunting is the same feeling as catching up with a friend over a glass of wine. We're just having a conversation. The difference is that when I'm talking to ghosts, the conversation is slightly more one-sided. Sometimes it takes a *lot* of questions to get an entity to share even a few words. But then again, I've been on dates where it was pretty much the same.

This fundamental idea that ghosts are, first and foremost, just trying to be heard, gets more complicated when it comes to places where people have experienced truly terrifying things. I've seen cases where ghosts genuinely are trying to scare people, or to hurt them. I've also investigated situations where the supernatural presence is a positive force, and the people love having the ghosts around. What's so interesting to me is that these two totally different experiences can be happening to people in the same family, who live together in the same house.

Believe it or not, that's the real story behind the home from *The Conjuring.*

There is no denying that the Perron family—the one whose experiences formed the basis for *The Conjuring*— went through an extended haunting in an eighteenth-century farmhouse in Harrisville, Rhode Island. Roger and Carolyn Perron, and their daughters Andrea, Nancy, Christine, Cindy, and April, felt the presence of the supernatural as part of their daily lives for almost ten years, the entire time they lived in that house, from 1970 to 1980.

That family lived with a lot of different ghosts in a very haunted, not always safe, house. It was investigated five times by paranormal experts Ed and Lorraine Warren (who also famously worked with the house from *The Amityville Horror* and the haunted doll from *Annabelle*). When they first arrived to investigate, Andrea Perron said, "They waited until the day before Halloween. Mrs. Warren said they thought the veil would be thinner and they'd have the best chance of seeing a manifestation. My mother looked at her and snickered, and said, 'Then every day is Halloween in this house.'"

The Conjuring, though it's loosely based on Andrea Perron's memoirs and Lorraine Warren's own recollections, doesn't really capture what that family went through. In real life, there was no devil-worshipping spirit possessing the women who lived in the home so they'd murder their kids, no haunted jewelry box, no ghost named Rory hiding in the crawl space. There wasn't even a crawl space in the actual house. We'll get more into the truth as we go, but it's important that you erase everything you think you learned about the Perrons from *The Conjuring* if we're going to talk about the family's actual experiences.

Andrea has been a friend for a long time, and she's always

said that the movie was nothing like what happened to them in the house, because—get this—what happened to them in the house was "a lot scarier." Scarier than unseen forces dragging adolescent girls around by their hair.

Take a second to let that sink in.

Carolyn Perron, the mother, has refused to come back to the house since she left in 1980, and the family's youngest daughter, April, passed away in 2017. Roger and the four living sisters came back to the house for the first time as a group for an episode on Season 4 of *Kindred*, and the family talked a lot about their memories of that period, and the experiences they had in the home. They were all in agreement that terrible, traumatic things had happened to them there. But they were also in agreement that they had a lot of happy supernatural experiences during that time as well.

Carolyn and the second youngest daughter, Cindy, got the worst of the abuse from the ghosts in that house. In Andrea's recollection, her mother was injured at least five times, including being impaled through the hip with a garden stake; stabbed with an invisible needle in the leg; and cut across the neck with a hand scythe thrown at her in the barn. Cindy almost drowned when she was held underwater in the bathtub by something unseen, and was nearly suffocated when she was trapped inside an old wooden box that wouldn't open, even though it didn't have a lock on it. The same thing happened to Christine in an antique trunk. The girls would get cornered inside closets with no way to get out. They would hear voices all the time, or suddenly go cold, only to turn around and see something otherworldly standing there.

But at the same time all those harrowing things were happening, the family was also having positive experiences with presences in the house, too. That's the part of the story that, in their view, was overlooked by both the movie and by the accounts from the Warrens themselves. Many of their brushes with entities in the home—especially Andrea's, Nancy's, and Roger's experiences—were happy ones. "I had plenty of interaction with spirits in that house, but it was always peaceful," Andrea said. "I felt protected." She thinks that's because she kept journals of what she was witnessing there, and was committing those accounts to memory. (I think it's a pretty solid theory. Remember Peg Dunn? Chip Coffey's reading of that situation was that Peg was being a prankster so that he'd be remembered and talked about after he'd passed away.)

"When we first moved in, my mother would walk through that house every single night and kiss all of us good night," Andrea said. "We all remember a woman who used to come through the house and do the same thing." She explained that all the girls felt a similar sensation, and that they all assumed it was their mother coming back in after they were asleep for one final check.

"Cindy's the one who said, 'That wasn't Mom, because Mom always smells like Ivory Soap and that lady smells like flowers and fruit.'"

The family also talked about Oliver Richardson, whom they believed was the son of the eighteenth-century family that built the house. Oliver died young, and his spirit played with April when the other sisters were at school. April had kept his existence from the Warrens, Andrea said, because she was fearful if she disclosed his presence, they would somehow force him to leave the house, and she loved him. (We couldn't verify Oliver's existence in our research, but that doesn't mean he wasn't there. One of the hardest parts of this work is finding records on children from centuries past. Their births and deaths were severely underreported because before modern medicine, their mortality rates were so high.)

Roger shared his experience with a woman in the house—not the same one, they believe, who would tuck the girls in at night—and his emotional connection with her. He described her as a gentle spirit who would greet him every day by touching him on the back. That's an experience I can personally validate, because when I was investigating the house for the show, I felt the exact same thing. There was a moment when I felt a hand caress my back, like the comforting touch of a mother. Normally, I hate being touched by ghosts. I hate being touched by any stranger, especially one I can't see. This instance was the one and only time when I thought, *This is actually pleasant.*

Of all the sisters, Cindy wanted to come back the least. She had a really hard time being in that home, even with her family, the cast and crew of the show, and the current homeowners all there together. But on the other hand, when the Perrons sold the house, Nancy was so reluctant to leave that she offered to stay and be the caretaker for the new owners. That's how much she loved that place.

During the séance that happened the final time the Warrens investigated the home, Carolyn Perron was thrown across a room while sitting in a chair and knocked unconscious. Still, even she has a somewhat positive view of those years. Carolyn was the one who titled Andrea's books. "She just crossed her arms and said '*House of Darkness House of Light.* It was both,'" Andrea said.

"I feel very much at home there and very comfortable in that environment," she explained. "It's the only place on earth that has ever felt like my permanent place. Everything else feels temporary. The farm is home."

So what really happened there? Honestly, I don't know.

The sisters say that they did sense those same spirits when they visited the home with us, and that they were making contact with them, even while Adam and I were there investigating and not finding much ourselves. If you look closely at the episode, you can see a moment where Cindy is shaking her head and mouthing the word "no," which she said was in response to someone unseen ordering her to go into the cellar, and then into the library. The day after she was at the house, Cindy returned to her home in Georgia. She reported feeling physically ill and found a huge bruise on the back of her leg she had no recollection of getting. Andrea believes Cindy's physical symptoms were retaliation for not doing what the ghosts had wanted her to do. Cindy has sworn to never go back to the house.

I don't have a good explanation for why the spirits that interacted so strongly with that family didn't appear for us, or for the home's new owners. Andrea said she got the sense that the ghosts were unsettled by all of the change and commotion in the house and didn't feel comfortable revealing themselves. My hope is that, over time, each new visit and investigation will reveal new information.

One thing I can tell you is that I personally had a hard time being in that space. Even though Adam and I didn't find any evidence of the spirits that the Perrons described, I'm still not convinced the house is completely safe. There's something in the farmhouse that has an affinity toward children, and it's not necessarily a nice affinity. We weren't able to confirm who was there, but we were able to gather that whoever they are, they made themselves known more to children than adults and we don't know why. Luckily, since it's practically in my backyard, the farmhouse is one of those places I'll definitely return to and keep trying to find out.

What we do know for sure is that Bathsheba Sherman, who has been maligned for decades as a devil worshipper who did unspeakable things to her own child, had nothing to do with that home. In the movie, she was an evil spirit who perpetuated a legacy of murder in the women who lived in the home after she did. In reality, she didn't even live in that house, and she *definitely* didn't murder anyone. There's no evidence or historical record to indicate she was anything but an ordinary woman who lived a normal life on a nearby homestead. That legend is a product of the investigations of the home by Ed and Lorraine Warren.

I want to be clear, though, that I respect and admire the Warrens very much. The work they've done and the strides they made in making the paranormal more mainstream helped to pave the path that I'm walking today. But the research I've done, and the information I've seen from the Harrisville Historical Society, have led me to believe they were wrong about Bathsheba. That poor woman has been blamed for nearly fifty years for things she had nothing to do with. She's been dead for centuries. She can't defend herself.

I really don't know where that information came from,

or how any of it happened. But the result of that mis-information was decades of what I believe is historical inaccuracy unintentionally presented as fact, both in the Warrens' work and (in a highly dramatized version) in *The Conjuring*, and it has had repercussions in real life. Bathsheba's gravestone in Harrisville has been stolen and defaced so many times that the Harrisville Historical Society had to permanently remove it from her burial site. And the house, of course, has become the target of so much tourist traffic—often unfriendly—that a former owner sued Warner Bros. Granted, that same person has gone on a personal crusade to disprove the home's haunted history, *even after* she spent years on the public record talking about those ghosts. She went as far as to invite *Ghost Hunters* in for an episode in Season 2 of that show. Did I mention she showed up screaming at us while we were filming our *Kindred Spirits* episode? Because she definitely did that, too.

The point of all this is that what happened with Bathsheba is a teachable moment. This is the ultimate example of why good research is so important, and why you *have* to do your homework and get your history right. The seventies and eighties saw a rash of people like the Warrens (such as Hans Holzer and Sylvia Browne), who were widely renowned for their new perspectives on the paranormal, but who had strictly defined ideas of what "the paranormal" was. I think that, with their unique perspective on the investigation, Ed and Lorraine were looking for someone to take the blame, and provide a clear explanation for what was happening.

To me, it was a sign of the times more than a purposeful spreading of misinformation. I grew up reading authors like the Warrens when I was a kid, and I took all of them at their word. It wasn't until later when I thought, *Wait a minute, maybe we shouldn't just run with these ideas.* Today, we're in a space where people are a little more skeptical about the paranormal. They're not dismissing it entirely, but they're not ready to embrace these ideas of sending things into the light, or the idea of demons and angels, as the only possible solution. Now, we have these amazing archives of newspapers and historical records online, and even more extensive resources at historical societies. We can go in and correct that kind of misinformation.

That's honestly what I love so much about ghost hunting. It's so interesting to me to actually find the history. We uncovered *so much* that we didn't have time to include it all in the show. For example, we looked into the seven dead soldiers so often mentioned in the house's lore, but couldn't find any evidence of them. We couldn't even find a record of any military activity in the area at all, not so much as an encampment. We did find that a man died of exposure in a snowstorm just outside the house, while his family was waiting inside for him, and evidence of a man who wandered drunk into the barn and died. There was a huge number of suicides in the area, more than any other case I've ever researched, but there was no discoverable evidence of the woman who was rumored to have hung herself in the barn, who many people suspect is the bent-neck lady depicted on the wall in the basement. There are rumors and whispers of a lot more deaths in and around that house, but there's no evidence of them. At that point, you're playing a game of telephone that goes back two hundred years. Eventually, the trail leads nowhere.

AN UNINVITED GUEST

For an episode of *Ghost Hunters*, we had gone to Essex County Prison in New Jersey to investigate. The abandoned prison was built in 1837 and closed in 1970, so there was a long span of time in which to build up negative energy in that space—especially since it had a gallows on site for prisoners sentenced to death by hanging.

By the time we visited, the building was in severe disrepair, and there were numerous reports of shadow figures, disembodied footsteps, and the jangling of unseen keys. At that time on the show, we had an uneven number of investigators, so sometimes one of us wouldn't have a partner for an investigation.

During my downtime, I had a brilliant idea: The cameraman could come investigate with me! I'd appear "alone" on camera, but you wouldn't have to be a rocket scientist to figure out that I wasn't actually alone, because someone was there to film me.

We headed down to the tunnels beneath the prison. I knew the complex had become a haven for homeless drug addicts, but the buildings we were investigating that night had been checked by security, who made certain there was no one inside them.

When we went down into the tunnels, it didn't really occur to me that we were out of bounds of that security clearance.

Eventually, I noticed what appeared to be a grate in the ceiling of the tunnel, that looked like it could be moved. And lucky me, there was a steel barrel nearby that I could stand on to get up there and see inside. Just then, I heard a noise above. My curiosity was piqued. Could it be an animal? Or maybe…a ghost?

What I didn't see coming was that I was going to jump on top of that barrel, lift the grate, poke my head through and come directly face to face with a man.

A man who was very surprised to see me.

A man whose face told me that I was an unwelcome guest. And that I was leaving. *Now.*

I jumped (fell) down, and walked (ran) out of the tunnels. Clearly, security hadn't gotten to that building.

Chapter 3

GHOST HUNTING IS A HOBBY, NOT A CAREER

THE QUESTION I get asked the most is how to get a job like mine, traveling the country in search of haunted experiences, making a living doing what most consider to be a very odd, very expensive weekend hobby.

The answer is: I have no idea.

There isn't a traditional path to finding a career in the paranormal. It started out as a hobby for me, too. I investigated for fun for years before I made anything at all from ghost hunting—in fact, investigating cases usually *cost* me money. When you're doing your own investigations, it's hard to have the resources to do them to the level you want to do them. If you're traveling to the location, that can be costly, and there's time off work to consider, on top of the expensive equipment a lot of people like to use. Investigating can be as simple as just using your phone's flashlight and recorder, but it's a lot less fun than seeing entities wave at you through a structured light sensor (SLS) camera.

I was not even thinking about making it a job back then. It was a long time before investigation of the supernatural became a sustainable life path for me. Thankfully, with *Kindred Spirits*, I can travel all over the country and spend days on end investigating and researching new information to utilize in those investigations. I never forget for a second that I am incredibly lucky to be able to do what I love, and to have a platform to share my ideas and my work with the world. There is no end to my gratitude about it.

But when I started out, I never dreamed this would become a job for me.

To be honest, I can't even identify a moment when I started looking for ghosts. They were always there. I come from a family of people who all have unique gifts, one of which is unintentionally moving into homes that later turn out to be haunted. My Auntie Roxi and Auntie Lizzie, my father's sisters, are both sensitive in certain ways. When my sister Becky was sixteen, she got encephalitis and ended up in a coma. I'll never forget my aunts coming into the hospital room to perform rituals over her. They chanted and meditated, then smudged the room with sage smoke even though smudging is *definitely* not allowed in hospitals. I was very much raised with that kind of belief in magic, and the power of energy and intention.

Imagine having that stuff happening around you as a kid. You're never going to be normal.

My dad has his own gifts, which he keeps very private. To this day, I still don't know the details of what he does pertaining to the supernatural. He's never discussed it with his sisters, or even my mother when they were married. I've just gotten bits and pieces of it. I think people call him to clear their houses of ghosts, but how or why he does it—or, honestly, whether it works—are total mysteries to me. That privacy might be because he's a physicist by trade, and his science mind is at odds with his paranormal leanings. The only thing I know for sure about what he does is that he's never going to discuss it.

When I was twelve, my dad once took me along on a case. At the time, I had no idea that he was doing anything like this. Our friends had this beautiful home in Petaluma, California, that they rented out, but it was plagued by troubles. Every time they leased it to a new tenant, things would go wrong. Deeply wrong. Tenants went crazy, smashing furniture and breaking down walls, completely destroying the place. They had three people in a row do that. Our friends were convinced the place was cursed or haunted. So once the last tenant had moved out, they called my dad in to see if he could lift whatever was going on there.

I remember clearly what happened. We rode there on my dad's motorcycle, and I knew the minute we walked in the door that something in the house was off. The place had a really weird vibe. My dad went upstairs to do something, and I decided to go downstairs into the basement. Alone.

And that's where I saw two red eyes staring at me.

I ran up the stairs, screamed for my dad, and told him what happened. I couldn't be in that house anymore after what I had seen. My mom came to get me, but he stayed behind to finish his work. He was there all night in the house by himself, with just a sleeping bag, a lantern, and a book. As far as we know, nothing ever happened in the house after that. To this day, I still don't understand what was going on there or what my dad did. He won't tell anybody. And what I saw easily could have been imagined by a freaked-out twelve-year-old kid who was making something out of the darkness. I'd have to go back to the home and investigate now to really get an answer. But it stands out in my memory as one of the scariest and weirdest moments I've ever had.

Still, though, and I can't emphasize this enough, there were a *lot* of weird moments. Mr. Green Jeans, as my aunts like to call the soldier who appeared outside the window of my house in Alameda, might have been the first ghost I saw as a kid, but he was far from the only one. We all had plenty of other supernatural experiences. One time, when I was very little, before I was in school, Auntie Roxi was babysitting me. I was trying to get her to keep playing a game she didn't want to play. We were in her bedroom—with "the closet everyone knew was haunted," as she describes it—and I kept pushing her to start again. Then, she said, a hanger on the knob of the closet door started to spin, slooooowly going all the way around the knob in a circle, so slowly that it couldn't possibly have been the wind. We both stared at it. Then, being four, I screamed and ran away.

If you saw the Season 3 episode of *Kindred Spirits* when a ghost train tried to run me down, you already know I still sometimes do that as an adult, too.

I was very goth in my early teen years, and then punk rock in high school, but more than anything, I was that girl who was *really* interested in ghosts. I would go to New Age stores around San Francisco all the time. My mom and I went to psychic fairs and to see Sylvia Browne speak (before she made those public predictions that later turned out to be false). All our exploration of different supernatural ideas gave me the first pieces of information that were the seeds of the theories I've developed about the paranormal in my career.

As I got older and more serious about paranormal research, I kept that passion mostly to myself. I'd talk about it a little bit, but I wasn't introducing myself to new coworkers by telling them I liked learning about dead people. Other than the times I would investigate with my dad or my aunts, I was a loner researcher who did my own thing and explored what I could around Northern California.

Once *Ghost Hunters* debuted, the amateur ghost hunters started coming out of the woodwork. That show followed The Atlantic Paranormal Society (TAPS), based in Warwick, Rhode Island. Soon after it first aired, investigation teams began popping up, and one started near me in Sacramento, where I was living at the time. I interviewed with them, and we really hit it off. They were the first people who weren't family with whom I investigated in a serious way. We would meet once a month at the library and go through case requests. There were so many, more than we could handle, because *Ghost Hunters* was so huge and people were openly talking about spirits and hauntings in a way they never had before. With all the case requests coming in, we'd do some preliminary screening by phone, and then have them fill out an in-depth questionnaire about the activity they were having. Afterward, we'd go through the case requests one by one, deciding who would do what.

Almost immediately, investigations started taking up all of my nonwork time. We would be on cases every weekend, driving hours to these homes and staying in little motels. It was so much fun, and we did it all just for the love of finding ghosts and helping people put their minds at ease. Back then, investigators still mostly subscribed to the idea that proof of a haunting was the only goal of an investigation. Either we'd find something and be able to explain it to the homeowners, or we'd figure out that it wasn't actually a haunting, and explain that to them. Back then, it was more, *This is the evidence we've caught. You're not crazy, this is really happening.* It wasn't, *What do we do to fix it?* We didn't take the next step in those investigations of trying to help resolve the problem, or trying to uncover the underlying causes of the haunting. It just wasn't discussed then. It was more about the thrill of the hunt, and of finding evidence that spirits were really there.

That was the first time I felt like I had finally found my people, that I wasn't the only weirdo in the room. It was so refreshing, and it felt like such an adventure.

One of the cases we investigated on that first team was in Sacramento. The family who called us in had a beautiful home in a nice neighborhood—but even though there was a real estate boom happening, they could not sell their house for anything. We went two or three times to investigate, and try to figure out what was going on.

That family had a son who had died a few years earlier in a car accident, and what's worse, the accident happened right at the edge of their property. The son's spirit was in the home, and he was unsettled and very angry that they were trying to leave. You could feel the vibe as soon as you walked in the house, and there were frequent signs of his anger, like doors slamming. The son's spirit had been relatively quiet there with his family, but when they wanted to move elsewhere, he wanted them to know that it was not okay by him.

At that time, it wasn't standard practice to keep in touch with people after we investigated their cases. I don't think I ever heard from them again—so I don't know what happened to the family, or whether we ever really fixed what was happening. Back then, we were just documenting the information. I wish we could go back and revisit that home. It's a perfect *Kindred Spirits* case— and it would be so nice to make sure we really gave them all the help they needed back in the day.

At the same time as I was working on those local cases, I started branching out with my haunted experiences. I traveled farther to visit bigger landmarks, like the Stanley Hotel in Estes Park, Colorado, the hotel that inspired Stephen King to write *The Shining*. The first time I visited the hotel, around 2007, was to attend a paranormal convention. That's where I first met Dave Schrader, host of Darkness Radio, who in a full-circle moment later hosted our *Haunted Salem: Live* television event in October 2019.

Dave was one of the first people to start hosting the kind of large-scale paranormal events that went beyond standard conferences and became social gatherings. "We started going from these little events with forty or fifty people" near the TAPS headquarters in Rhode Island, Dave said, "to where we'd have three hundred people at the *Queen Mary*, or the Stanley, or Eastern State Penitentiary. All these great big haunted locations that were perfect for this type of group."

As Dave explained it, the events he'd produce, which brought burgeoning paranormal stars around the country to notoriously haunted locations, weren't really happening before the early 2000s. "There were these big paranormal conferences at Penn State called Univ-Con. It was basically lecture after lecture from these big ghost hunters like Lorraine Warren, Lou Gentile, John Zaffis," he said, "but it had never been [my kind of] traveling road show.

"I thought we were going to need to keep looking for new locations," to maintain people's interest, Dave said, "but every time we'd book it they'd sell out." I was right there with all those ghost fans. The events would have parties where you could meet and talk to the paranormal celebrities, then hear lectures by them during the day and investigate haunted locations with them at night. It was such a full-circle moment for me when I started Strange Escapes, my paranormal travel company, and began hosting events like that on my own, because meeting people back in the day had meant so much to me.

Branching out into the larger paranormal community

was a total game changer for me. At that first paranormal conference (paracon), I connected with people
who shared my passion for investigation and research.
But more than that, I realized I wasn't completely alone
in my ideas, and not just about how to talk to ghosts.
These people believed ghosts were real entities we live
among every day, just like I did. For a long time, I didn't
talk about that stuff in any in-depth way. Sure, people
have their casual beliefs about ghosts. But mine was more
like, *Not only do I believe in ghosts, but I'm into them so much
that I go to haunted places in the dark by myself to look for them.*
Try digging into the really clear EVPs that you just got
inside a haunted battleship at a dinner party full of non-
paranormal folk and see the kind of looks you get.

Not at the Stanley. There, I had one of my crazi-
est paranormal experiences, and a whole convention of
fellow ghost geeks to talk about it with.

I was investigating in the hotel's carriage house, which
was off the side of the main building, and used for storage.
There were so many rumors about that space—that it had
been used to hold Native Americans captive, for one—
but no way to verify what had actually happened there.
It wasn't open to the public, so it was a novelty that we
got to be in that space at all. Basically, it was a dirt-floor
barn that held old mattresses. We were all sitting on one
side of the room, and we were asking whoever was there
to come closer and talk to us. All of a sudden, I heard feet

running across the dirt. It was so loud and pronounced that there was no way it could have been anything else. We all jumped because it was like someone was running right at our faces.

We also had a spirit box running, which is a modified radio that amplifies paranormal voices. It was the first time I had ever used a Frank's Box, and the first time I met Frank Sumption, who invented the prototype that became the spirit boxes we use today. Out of the box, clear as day, we heard, *Pray on your own.* Whatever was in there with us started pacing back and forth in the doorway with pronounced footsteps, like it was waiting for us to leave.

The Stanley is a space I would love to go back to at some point, to try to figure out what's really there, and shed some light on what I saw that night. The hotel used to embrace its haunted history and legacy of creepy legends, but not anymore. The owners have moved away from that kind of tourism, and no longer allow paranormal-related events and investigations there. Now their focus is more on live music, illusionists, and magicians. I haven't been able to go back in a lot of years, but I'm hoping one day that door will reopen for me, so I can get to the bottom of who or what is there.

A lot of people were at these events because they were amateur investigators, but many of the attendees were also just there because they were fans of *Ghost Hunters*. It was the first reality show where you could watch real investigators search for actual supernatural evidence. Now it seems totally commonplace—turn on the television on any given night and you can find people searching for Bigfoot or Atlantis—but back then it was a bona fide phenomenon.

To handle the volume of investigation requests that TAPS would get once the show started airing, Jason (Jay) Hawes and Grant Wilson, cofounders of the organization, started the TAPS Family network. Paranormal groups around the world that shared similar investigative methodologies could apply to become affiliates of TAPS, and have nearby cases referred to them. Our group in Sacramento was part of the TAPS Family, which had something like 150 member organizations around the United States by then.

Things started to sour a little bit between me and some of the Sacramento group because I became friendly with Jay and Grant, and they couldn't understand why these famous guys would choose to talk to a newbie member of their team, rather than the people who had been around the longest. In all honesty, I just sent Grant a Myspace friend request. (Remember when you could meet people that way?) He accepted and wrote me a message saying, "Welcome to the madness." We just started chatting. We have very similar interests in art and music, as well as similar theories on the paranormal.

I was working a side gig as a producer on a paranormal podcast at the time that had grown out of the TAPS Family network. A bunch of the paranormal investigation groups that were part of the network would contribute content. I wasn't a host—I was booking guests like spiritual medium Derek Acorah; John Zaffis, founder of the Paranormal Research Society of New England; and professional skeptic James Randi, who offered the One Million Dollar Paranormal Challenge to anyone who could produce concrete evidence of having a supernatural ability.

I had also moved from just attending paracons to presenting at them about the dynamics in paranormal investigation groups. Out of curiosity, I had started collecting information about when and how groups formed, sending out surveys through the TAPS Family network and through Myspace. Eventually I had responses from over five hundred groups throughout the country.

I was trying to figure out why people were investigating, what their methods were, what their belief systems were, what kind of education levels they had, how the group structures worked. Anything about what they were doing. What I found was fascinating: Almost all of those groups had started after *Ghost Hunters* premiered, and most of the members of these new groups hadn't so much as read a book about the paranormal before they started. Most of them were basing their investigations completely on what they were watching on TV.

I've always been passionate about research, having built such a historical foundation from all that time in libraries when I was young, that I felt like this was a little niche I could carve out for myself. In the 2000s, we were basically experiencing a revival of the Victorian era Spiritualism movement, where people's evening entertainment was trying to communicate with ghosts. These current-day investigators may have all been inspired by what they were seeing on television, but there was so much more to know about the supernatural than that.

In those talks, I would give them some historical context of where ghost hunting came from, and some of what I felt were the more credible books on the subject. I'd recommend titles like *ESP, Hauntings and Poltergeists: A Parapsychologist's Handbook* by Loyd Auerbach and *Communicating with the Dead: Reach Beyond the Grave* by Jeff Belanger.

At the same time I was starting to present at conferences and working on the podcast, Jay and Grant were producing a paranormal radio show called *Beyond Reality Radio* that was syndicated all over the country, and they wanted a hands-on producer. They started noticing who I was booking as guests on my show, and they asked if I'd be interested in coming on board with them. We finally met in person when they came out to San Francisco to film an episode, even though we'd been working together for a while by that point.

They introduced me to Kris Williams, who was new to their team on *GH*. She and I hit it off really well. A few months later, they all came back out to the Bay Area to film another episode. At that time, *Ghost Hunters International* was aggressively asking me to do their show, and I kept turning it down. I had a good job in health care with benefits and insurance. I wasn't leaving all that to go chase ghosts in Europe. But when they heard I was being recruited, Jay and Grant invited me to come do *Ghost Hunters.*

This sounds like a big mistake, I remember thinking to myself. *Leaving my great job to go hunt ghosts on a reality television show seems like the most idiotic, irresponsible thing I could do.*

But by then, my ex and I were separated, and I was at loose ends. I didn't know what my next chapter would be. Jay and Grant called me again and asked me to come on a case they were filming in California. "Just try it out and see what you think," they said. Kris had become a good friend by that point, and the role they were recruiting me for was to be her investigative partner. "I was pretty loud about wanting Amy on the show," Kris said recently, "because I figured if we're going to get another person, and I'm going to be paired up with them, it would be nice if it was somebody I was actually friends with."

So I went. I'll never forget it. My first case was Clovis Avenue Sanitarium in Clovis, California, and my second, right afterward, was the USS *Hornet* in Alameda, where

I'd lived in my first haunted house. The way the episodes aired, they flip-flopped it so it looked like my first case was in Alameda, but it was really the former sanatorium in Clovis.

It's strange to think back on those first episodes, because the paranormal experiences don't stand out to me nearly as much as the nerves I felt being on camera for the first time. Think about it like the first day at a new school, where everyone there is already a tightly knit group and everyone knows what they're doing *way* more than you do. I was trying to keep up with them, and trying to fit into the group dynamic—but at the same time, I was hyperaware of the filming, and of trying not to mess up any footage.

Also, and I say this with love, not everyone on the team was glad to have me there. Steve Gonsalves, especially, was wary of me. He was very protective of TAPS, and of the way they did things, and he didn't know me at all. I can't blame him—I was just some girl from California. He was the hardest to win over, but it was worth the work. He's still one of my very best friends to this day.

I had a lot of investigations under my belt by then, but I still felt relatively new—and I had certainly never done anything on the scale of *Ghost Hunters* before. Determined not to let the situation get the best of me, I decided to treat that first case at Clovis Sanitarium like any other. Go in, ask questions, investigate as well as I could (and, you know, try not to make an ass of myself on camera). I tried to just be myself and act like the crew wasn't there. If you've ever been on camera like that, you know that when the lens is pointed at you, it's easier said than done.

It helped that I was with Kris. She was also fairly new, having been on the show just about a year at that point. I remember one time we were chatting and joking, just being our normal selves, and it felt so comfortable. Then I turned my head, and saw the camera, and completely freaked out. *That's millions of eyes*, I thought to myself. *Millions.* Then, from the basement, Kris and I heard a softball-size piece of concrete get thrown across the room above.

That definitely brought my attention back to the ghosts.

The house, originally a mansion that became a sanatorium where hundreds of people died, was definitely haunted. On that same investigation, Grant experienced what he called the loudest disembodied voice he'd ever heard. It was a man saying *I like the one with the hat*, referring to Jay. The home had been empty for decades before being turned into a haunted house. Todd Wolfe, the owner who called in TAPS (as well as several other paranormal shows like *Ghost Adventures* and *The Dead Files*) tried to turn it into a bed-and-breakfast called Wolfe Manor—with the ghosts as an added draw—but the building was eventually condemned and torn down.

After those two cases, Jay and Grant said, "We're

headed to San Diego, do you want to come?" So I left my car at my grandmother's house and went with them. And I really never went home after that. I was on the road with *Ghost Hunters* for seven years.

At my exit interview at my job, I told the human resources person that I was leaving to go hunt ghosts on a reality television show. I remember that woman looking at me like I was absolutely insane. But that was the beginning. I had a hunch that if I did *Ghost Hunters*, other avenues would open up for me. I thought maybe the show would last a season or two—boy, did I underestimate that—and that I was on the path to something else. That show cast me down a road where I ended up spending a lot of time in New England, where I eventually met the father of my child, and now I have Charlotte. Saying yes that day was the catalyst for opening up a whole new part of my life that never would have happened otherwise.

"When Amy came in, I finally felt like I belonged," Kris said. "It helped that she had been at it for a lot longer than I had off television.

"It took us a little while to find our balance, but once we did, we were good," she added. I loved the history and research part of investigation—and I later took on the role of primary researcher on *Ghost Hunters*—but Kris was the primary researcher on the show at the time. I would add to her work when I could, but it was her role to delve into the history and look through records to help guide our live investigations. In the beginning, I was more into the tech side of things. We both had our roles and we'd play off each other. One thing we'd often go back and forth on was our level of skepticism. Kris was always *much* more skeptical than I was, always looking for every possible explanation, and later doubting what she saw. I was more ready to believe in the weirdness because of what I had already experienced in my life. We'd see an eight-foot shadow walking in a room, and would both acknowledge what we experienced, but later on she'd be less sure that she saw anything at all.

"Amy's much more of a believer and I am not as much," she said. "I've always been very big on fact and records and solid proof, and the paranormal isn't something I feel that you can solidly prove. Usually, we'd walk into a case and I'd rattle off the history, and we'd talk about the claims in that room. Then based on the claim, she'd explain what we were using for tech and why we were using it."

I joined the show at its most popular point. Before streaming television and DVRs, people watched the show religiously, every Wednesday night at 9 p.m. We'd average almost three million viewers per episode, and were consistently a top-rated show. People would wait in line for hours to get the *Ghost Hunters'* cast autographs at events. Being on the show with those guys on the first few cases, no one knew who I was, so I saw up close the way they'd be treated like rock stars. We'd be unloading gear at a hotel, and people would come running and screaming to see them there. I was just like, *What did I get myself into?*

I did seven seasons of *Ghost Hunters*, 119 episodes. It was such an insane ride. We'd stay up all night investigating, sleep all day, then do it all over again. I always tell people that traveling with TAPS was like being in a band, without any of the sex, drugs, or rock and roll.

If I hadn't said yes and taken that crazy chance, I would probably be in Northern California, still ghost hunting as a hobby and still very much in love with it. I think I made that leap because it was perfect timing for me to get away from my past in Sacramento, and to start a new chapter in my life. But I never did any of it with the intention of becoming famous or being on television. That's what gives me pause when I see these videos of people doing dangerous things, like attempting an exorcism or a "devil summoning." They are playing with things they don't understand, and it seems like they are doing it to try to get their fifteen minutes of fame. But those actions could have deeply dangerous consequences.

A lot of the time, being on the show was great. But it could get really stressful, too. There was definite tension on the team, and occasional infighting, which was mostly people trying to protect their roles and assert seniority. There were also constant threats I was going to be fired. But the more negativity I got, the more it fueled me to keep going. "It's an odd dynamic because everybody's working together, and they're basically living together," Kris said. "It was pretty full-on."

She and I also read way too much criticism people said about us on the internet, and took it close to heart. Nowadays, I'm used to people being…let's just say "less than nice" online, but back then we took it all very seriously. Though there were so many kind people saying great things about us and the show, we listened to the negative a lot more than the positive.

That's part of why I never feel I have a good answer when people ask me how to become a professional investigator. There are maybe a few dozen of us who do this as a full-time job, and I hear more people than that tell me at any one meet-and-greet event they want to have a job like mine. I especially hear it from teenagers who dream of becoming "real" ghost hunters. I wish I had a foolproof way to help guide them into this kind of life. But it took years of really, really hard work, and being told by basically everyone in my life that I was crazy, before I made it happen. And even at this point, I don't know if it will last forever for me. That's why I always say it's a hobby and not a career. If you get really lucky, it might become a job for you. But honestly, you should have a backup plan.

The TAPS team kept me on my toes, that's for sure. But the good always outweighed the bad. I am incredibly appreciative of the opportunity they gave me, and I'm still in touch with a lot of them. We came a long way together, and came out better on the other side. Kris is still a great friend of mine. She's the most fiercely loyal person I've ever met, and the truest-to-her-word New Englander you will ever encounter. She went on to *Ghost Hunters International.* After *GH* ended in 2016, Grant started a revival of *Ghost Hunters* on a new network, and Jay, Steve, and Dave Tango moved on to *Ghost Nation.*

When Adam started on the show in 2010, coming over from *Ghost Hunters Academy,* we immediately clicked. There was none of the competition or tension I had felt with others in the field. We were just completely ourselves, and we didn't worry about anything else.

One year, we were on the road for three hundred days. On each episode, we did at least two investigations— so we're talking about hundreds of investigations over the years. And each time we'd find evidence, the most common EVP we'd get would be *Help me.* Hundreds of times I had to walk away from spirits who needed help, but I wasn't able to give it to them. Since I've changed the focus of my investigations to find the *why* and not just the *what,* I've seen cases where ghosts needed help because they didn't know where they were, or what had happened to them. Sometimes they wanted help with unfinished business. Sometimes they just wanted to be remembered. But then, I would hear spirits crying, and I wouldn't have the time to help them. We had a production schedule to keep, and planes to catch because we were due at our next location. That's when I really started switching gears. I couldn't keep leaving them the way I had to leave the nurses at Waverly Hills.

That day broke both mine and Adam's hearts, in the same way. That's why, ultimately, we both thought it could work for us to go off together and find our own path in the paranormal. It was time to go put our philosophies into practice.

THE GHOSTS OF THE BILTMORE HOTEL

Early in *Ghost Hunters*, I was checking into the Providence Biltmore, which is now the Graduate Providence, in Rhode Island. We would stay there all the time for the show. They gave me my key at the front desk, and the bellboy went up with me because I had been on the road for four weeks, so I had a ton of luggage.

We got to my room and we tried the key. It worked, but the deadbolt was locked from the inside. We tried a couple of times, and the deadbolt was still engaged. He was like, *Hm, that's strange.* So we knocked, and there was no one in there.

The bellboy went downstairs to get a master key. I was standing there at the door, waiting for him to come back, when I heard the phone start ringing in that room. It just rang and rang and rang. He came back after a long time, saying he couldn't find the maintenance guy with the master key.

"I heard them calling and calling to see if there was someone in there," I said.

"I didn't tell anybody what was happening," he said. "No one's called."

I was like, *What?*

So he said, "Let me go look for someone again." And I said, "You know what? Let's just try my key again." That time, the key worked. We opened the door, and we couldn't believe what we saw.

Every drawer was pulled out, in the bureau, in the nightstand, everywhere. The closet door was wide open.

It was *so weird.*

We had both tried that door. He looked at me and he was as white as a ghost. He had seen the deadbolt. We'd both seen the deadbolt. You'd push the door open and the deadbolt would stop it. I was like, "Well, I can't wait to stay *here* for the next week and a half."

Nothing happened after that, but it was definitely a rush.

When ghosts move furniture like that, I think it's just a sign, a way of saying, *Hey, we're here. Just letting you know.* I would do that. Can you imagine, like in *Poltergeist*, with all those chairs stacked? Leaving things out of the way that aren't supposed to be out of the way. It's such a clear signal something you can't see is there—you're thinking, *I know I didn't do that.* Except for me. I actually do leave cabinets open all the time. It drives people crazy.

Chapter 4
YOU'RE NOT CROSSING ANYONE OVER

(Ever)

PART OF THE reason that I felt ready to leave *Ghost Hunters* is that I had just had my daughter, and a life spent mainly on the road wasn't manageable for me anymore. But I had also reached a point on the show where I had learned and grown as much as I felt I could, and I was ready for a change. It wasn't anything against the people I worked with—we had all reached a good place by then—but wanting to be home with my daughter, coupled with the fact that I felt like I needed to expand my horizons, was enough for me to close that chapter.

Kindred Spirits wasn't even a dream when I left *Ghost Hunters*. But when Adam and I came up with the concept and an opportunity came knocking—an opportunity with significantly less travel and a schedule we were able to control—we both knew what we wanted to do. There was more work to be done. I've said it before, and I'll keep saying it until I can't anymore: Ghosts are people, too. To me, that doesn't just mean we find out who they are and why they're still here to help them move on and find peace. To me, that means respecting their free will—to the extent that they still have it—and most important, respecting their personal beliefs.

That's why I will never try to cross anyone over, and I will never support the idea that it's okay to try to do so.

The idea of crossing someone over or telling a person to "go into the light" has always seemed dismissive to me. We're not listening to them, we're not trying to help them, we're just walking in and telling them what to do. Why do we have the right or the power to decide that for someone else?

When I hear someone do that, I always just think, *You don't even know what's happening over there.* "Go ahead, you can go into the light," they say. I've heard it so many times. It just seems so presumptuous to walk in and start talking to these ghosts like they're three years old, like there was this big shining light behind them the whole time and they just never thought it might be a good idea to go have a closer look. What if there is no light? What if there isn't anything? The reality is, we just don't know. The vast majority of living people have no idea what happens after you die, or what the other side is like at all. (The exceptions, of course, are those who have had near-death experiences or people, like Chip Coffey, who can actually communicate with the other side.)

I love the idea of helping someone who has, whether by choice or by circumstance, stayed behind. My theory—and it really is just a theory, because there is no absolute way to prove any of this—is that people stay behind because they have a reason to. There's something they didn't feel they could leave. It's the classic idea of unfinished business. To me, if you help them with what they need help with and get their message across, they'll hopefully feel like they can move on. You're not doing the work of moving them on for those ghosts. You're helping them do the work so they can make their own choices.

Before I thought better of it, I totally subscribed to the theory that the goal of paranormal investigation was to first find evidence of ghosts, and second, move them on. If I got a good scare out of it, even better. I'm not trying to do that anymore. I've seen that ghosts exist with my own eyes, and I've been scared plenty enough to last a lifetime. At some point, I just thought to myself, *Why are we so egotistical to think we know what they need?* That's the point when I started asking them what they needed, and I genuinely began listening, because I wanted to help.

When Adam and I came up with the idea for *Kindred Spirits*, we wanted to tell the story of every spirit we encountered. We wanted to figure out who they were and, even more, why they would still be here. And almost every time, we've found a reason.

"I think we've brought a compassion level to the field that was always there, but shows didn't necessarily focus on it because they didn't think it was fun to watch," Adam Berry said. "I think there's something to treating the entities with respect, understanding, and empathy." He describes our style like we're guests at a party where we didn't know anyone else. "You wouldn't walk in saying 'HEY, TALK TO ME.' You'd walk in and say 'Hi, this is who I am. This is why we're here. How are you?'"

On Season 2 of *Kindred Spirits*, Delanne and Wayne asked us to come investigate their home in Somersworth, New Hampshire. They felt as though their three kids were being threatened by a dark presence in the home. Both of their sons experienced the feeling of something choking them in the night, and their daughter saw a dark shadow of a man in her bedroom. Their home wasn't safe, they felt, and they wanted to know what was happening and how to fix it.

The home was close to the previous residence of Joseph Kelley, an infamous murderer, who slit the throat of a teller in the local bank over a century ago. Because of the seemingly malicious nature of the haunting, we thought it might have been Kelley. We also thought it might have been the spirit of Delanne's brother, who had passed away many years ago. But when we attempted to speak to them, neither one responded.

We had another lead, though. Wayne had uncovered a gravestone in the backyard of the home, buried four feet beneath the earth. The stone belonged to Hollis B. Corbett, a World War I veteran who'd died in 1946. I researched him, and uncovered the gravestone order form his wife had filled out over seventy years ago. The stone over his grave in the cemetery, though, didn't reflect what she had written. It said "Hollie B. Corbett."

I don't know about you, but if my gravestone had a typo on it, I would be *pissed*.

Once we found that information, we had a solid lead to pursue at that night's investigations. We talked to Mr. Corbett about his daughter, who had died young, which explained why he was so interested in Delanne and Wayne's daughter. As for the sons, we think they may have been experiencing sleep paralysis. On the episode, I spoke to a psychologist who specializes in sleep disorders, who confirmed their symptoms were in line with that particular issue.

We also got some EVPs that indicated that he might not be so happy about his gravestone being incorrect. When I asked him if he had died at age forty-nine, he didn't waste any time in letting me know I got the math wrong. *Forty...eight*, he replied.

With this information, Adam and I were pretty sure

we knew what needed to happen to allow Mr. Corbett to find some peace. That gravestone from the backyard—which had been salvaged from a rubble pile by the home's previous owner—needed to go to the cemetery where it belonged. Delanne and Wayne were so relieved to know the entity in their home wasn't malicious. "Hollis, I know you've been trying to communicate and I never knew until now what you wanted," Delanne said. "Now that I know I'm going to make sure that it happens for you. I'm going to make sure that your stone gets where it belongs. We're your family now and we're going to take good care of you."

"We as humans in our own lives have reasons to do certain things," Adam said. "If we want something, we get it, because we need it. Why would that change in the afterlife? If someone's still around because they had unfinished business and there was a reason for their existence beyond this realm, why not try to figure out what that is and give it to them?"

John E. L. Tenney, a scholar of the paranormal and occult who often comes to Strange Escapes events with other "weirdos," as he lovingly calls people like us, believes that the idea of crossing people over is impossible simply because of human psychology. "We have difficulty communicating and understanding the ideas of physical people that are sitting across from us," he said, "much less trying to determine the means, motives, thoughts and desires of an unseen and invisible person or what was a person."

My personal belief is that there is far too much we don't know about the afterlife to try to tell anyone what they should be doing with themselves in it. We don't know what plane those entities exist on; we don't know how long they've been there or how long they intend to stay; we don't know whether they want to move on at all. More than that, John said, we can't rightly make claims about why people should go into the light because we don't know anything about that person's beliefs. "If they carry anything over with them that remains tied to their physical spirituality," he said, "we have no idea what they believe spiritually." So if a person is trying to use a Judeo-Christian way of helping a spirit exit—as in, telling them to go into "the light"—there's inherently a problem there. "You don't have any idea if that person was Mormon or Buddhist or Seventh-day Adventist," he added. "Why would they listen to you? To use biblical references or religious texts that you think would apply doesn't mean that it's going to apply to them."

Most cultures have a version of heaven that a spirit can move to, but the concept of "the light" wasn't always associated with heaven. It was brought to the forefront of spiritual thinking by Emanuel Swedenborg in the 1700s, John explained. "He talked about there being levels to reality, that this is only one realm of existence, and that there's one above it, and one above that. They get spiritually more progressed until they reach what could be considered the 'transcendent universal mind' in which individual spirit rejoins with its original source.

"When spiritualism took over in the 1800s in America, one of the biggest influences on that idea of the light was Andrew Jackson Davis," he added, who wrote a book about the "summer land." "It was a bright, always eternally sunshine-filled world that spirits go to. Him being eloquent enough to put down the ideas of summer land, this bright-lit heaven that spirits go to, really caught fire in the States and has completely taken hold since."

In the same way that we can't know their personal beliefs, the living also can't know the exact circumstances of an entity's existence on this plane, or what its journey has been after death. John believes it's possible that ghosts continue to grow and evolve over time the same way we do, even if they died young. "Everything in nature evolves," he said. "So when you die and fifty or a hundred years goes by, are you still the same person that you were when you died? Or did your ideas about the nature of reality and what happens after death change after you actually died?" By that thinking, you wouldn't be talking to a fifteen-year-old who died a hundred years ago. You'd be talking to someone who's 115. "You can only hypothesize, but it seems like a very good idea that once you have learned to experience the universe outside of the physical realm, your concepts on spirituality, on the nature of reality, on life and death, will have changed because you are no longer worried about dying."

(You could also be dealing not with the conscious spirit of a person, but with residual energy that doesn't have consciousness anymore. John calls that "a recording of a person." In that instance, no amount of talking will help because the entity can't understand you.)

Personally, I've seen spirits present in both ways. I think John's theory that spirits evolve makes total sense—but as I've investigated over the years, I've seen indications that they can appear in all different ages and forms.

The important thing to remember when we're theorizing about ghosts is that we don't even know what ghosts are in the technical sense. One day, there could be solid evidence leading to proven conclusions, and a concrete scientific explanation of why they're here. That day is not today, but it could be on the horizon. For all we know, there could be some kind of quantum physics time warp happening and that's why they appear at all different ages and in all different times. The age issue raises really interesting questions because of the inconsistencies in when and how they appear.

For our first-ever case on *Kindred Spirits*, we went to a home in Little Meadows, Pennsylvania. Catherine and her daughter Mary were living in a cabin deep in the woods, and they felt their home was haunted. Mary sometimes woke up with scratches all over her legs. Catherine came home one day to find a light fixture had been torn from the wall, leaving shattered glass and wood shards everywhere. Furniture moved for no reason. Once, Catherine woke up with a shadow figure, the size of a child, standing over her. They definitely did not feel safe in their home.

Catherine thought it might have been family members—her son-in-law had died unexpectedly, and her own son, Adam, had died in infancy at just four days old. "If it's not family," Catherine questioned, "why did they choose my home?"

The property's former owner, Fred Ashcraft Jr., had had a daughter named Lucinda who died at age three in the most horrible way imaginable. She walked directly into a moving blade at the family sawmill, and was cut in half. Just absolutely heartbreaking. It hit me especially hard because Charlotte was that little girl's age when I visited the home.

We pursued many different avenues of investigation for this case that didn't make it to air. We thought there might be soldiers from nearby battlefields, but there was no record of military activity on the property. We found what we suspected was a Native American burial mound, and brought in a shaman who didn't find any evidence of lingering indigenous spirits.

When we asked Catherine to sit in on the investigation,

she said, "Adam, if you're here, I feel you here every night." We heard a clear EVP: *Adam*. When we asked how old he was: *thirty-three*. "Adam would have been thirty-three this year," Catherine said. We had no idea. But we all had chills. "I always knew he was here," Catherine said.

Still, we weren't convinced that all the activity was coming from a loving family member. We thought Lucinda might be in the home, but we were having trouble getting in touch with her. Finally, I asked, "Are you lost?" And we got back, *I am*. "Are you a little girl?" *Yes*. And when we asked for a name: *Lucy*.

It was so much to process, the idea that the spirit of a scared little girl was in that home and didn't know where to go or what to do. One of the things the women had noticed was activity on a toy bench on the porch. It had a little circular saw blade attached to it, which could be spun by a hand, and would often spin on its own even when no one was nearby. But why did her infant son linger in her home, aging into a thirty-three-year-old man, when the little girl stayed three forever? We don't know definitively. It could have to do with the trauma surrounding her death, but it could also be that spirits can choose to exist in a state they choose. John Tenney thinks it's possible that as time progresses, even as a spirit, "you would learn things if you do continue on that path of growing and becoming informed." Maybe Adam wanted to learn and grow, so he chose to age. And maybe little

Lucy didn't get to have the rest of her childhood, so she wanted to stay a child forever. Questions like this are the reason I love investigating. There are always new things to learn, and new ideas to ponder.

"Lucinda if you're here, if that's you in my room, you can come out into the rest of the house and join us if it makes you happy and comfortable," Catherine said. "And if you see my son, feel free to interact with him." Since we left, Catherine said that she hasn't experienced any activity she feels is threatening. That's why I so strongly believe in the method that Adam and I use on *Kindred Spirits*. Because I've seen it work so many times.

There are so many things about life *and* the afterlife that I don't know. In all honesty, I don't even know what a ghost is in absolute terms. I work completely on theories and experiences (and I have plenty of those), but I don't have any concrete facts about what paranormal entities are or why they're here. What I do know is, I am capable of digging up actual information about moments in history that could have to do with activity happening in a location.

What people who haven't done in-depth investigations before don't usually realize is that getting to the bottom of a mystery like that is a *lot* of work. It involves multiple nights of investigating, tracking down and talking to people who have connections to the case, and spending hours upon hours going through old records in libraries and historical societies. It also involves asking a ton of questions in dark rooms, with the risk of going down the wrong rabbit hole and having to start all over again.

But once you do get that name or event, or something triggers activity that makes you certain you're on the right path, you can start building on it. When you find the answer, whatever it might be that the spirit or person is trying to convey to you, it's huge. It's such a rush, because you've solved the puzzle, but at the same time you know that you've helped to alleviate this claim. Many times the ghosts will leave or the activity will greatly subside afterward. If someone calls us because they don't feel safe in their home, and the things making that person feel unsafe no longer happen after we've done our work, I call that a win. I don't know if the ghost moves on, or where it goes. I *do* know that as I saw this method work time and time again, I became certain this was the right path for me. I've never looked back to those old ways.

Fans and critics frequently ask me how I know for certain that I've helped people in the long term. I definitely don't know if I have in every single case, but a lot of people from past cases do keep in touch with me. They'll check in and let me know how things are going, and whether there has been more activity since we investigated. Those people are often my biggest defenders on social media. When people try to say I'm not doing anything positive for people, or that I'm taking advantage of them when they need a solution, someone I've assisted in the past will pipe up and say "Actually my life changed after that" or "They were the only people who could help me when I had no one else to go to."

Delanne and Wayne are two of these people. When the haters come out on social media, they have often popped up in my defense, saying that they feel their home is a safer place now that they helped their ghost find his resolution. That makes it all worth it to me. There will always be people saying terrible things on the internet— but if folks say they feel safer and more protected, and that they're willing to talk about it publicly after we've worked with them, that makes all the difference to me.

James Gagliano, a co-executive producer on *Kindred Spirits*, is the person who's primarily responsible for helping us choose the final candidates for investigation. He has the most contact with these people who are inviting us into our homes, outside of Adam and me. "I think what Amy and Adam offer is kind of like a twofold service," he said. On one hand, we're coming in and providing supernatural answers as best we can. "But also, they're coming in and they're meeting with people who I think don't really have a lot of other people to talk to about this stuff, or a lot of other places to go. Amy and Adam come in, and listen to them, and believe them, and help them. When you combine those answers with that understanding and acceptance, I've seen it with my own eyes, it's really a helpful thing for a lot of these people."

In the future, my thoughts on the best way to investigate, and my research style, could evolve. For now, I feel with certainty that this is what gets the best results. I've seen it work too many times to doubt it. That's why I've started putting together lectures and workshops on digging deep into research, and techniques for this style of investigation. The more investigators I can get on board with this idea, the more of these unsettled spirits we can help. I love that so many people in the field are latching on to this method, and really trying to talk *to* spirits, and help them, rather than talk *at* them, and just gather evidence and leave.

"We're like ghost therapists," Adam said. "It's funny to say that, but that's really what it is. And we found out that we got more information doing that than not, and we just kept going in that direction because when you get results you don't regress." We always try different things (I'll talk more in the next chapter about some of the more unusual investigative methods we have used) but it's always on this path of using research and talking to ghosts with respect.

Adam and I both believe *Kindred Spirits* has had such a warm reception in the paranormal field because it's the first show to really lead with empathy, and focus on ghosts as people. "We were definitely the first TV show to demonstrate that kind of investigating, with a beginning, middle, and an end, with that kind of heart and history and information," he added. "Now, a lot of people have adopted that—what's the resolution, not just the scare factor? Some of the longest running shows have flipped the script."

The other reason I don't agree with moving people on? I've seen that it doesn't work.

I remember so clearly the moment when it hit me that maybe we weren't crossing spirits over the way we thought we were. I never personally attempted to cross anyone over, but I had known a lot of people who did, so I had a lot of faith in the idea. I just thought that's how things were done, especially since a lot of early investigators whose books I read, and whom I learned from, subscribed to the practice. I just never questioned it. And then once, in maybe 2007, I was investigating in Gettysburg, Pennsylvania, and I got clear evidence that the practice hadn't worked.

The year before, a good friend of mine, who's also an investigator, had been in that same home and believed he'd crossed spirits over while he was there. He had a lot of credibility, too: He had worked with the church before, and I had personally sat in with him at times when I felt like he was crossing things over. But the people in that house, when I spoke to them a year after this man had been inside and done his work, said that the activity had only gotten worse. So it dawned on me: *If he's not able to cross them over, then what's actually happening?*

After that, I just noticed the trend. I started asking around when we investigated things. I would find cases all the time where people would say they brought in a priest, or a shaman, or a psychic. Someone would come in and claim to have cleansed their home and removed the energy, and then they'd leave. Not only would the activity not go away, but things would intensify. Pairing that with the idea that over the years the most common EVP I get is *Help me* (well, it's probably tied with *Get out* for the top spot), I put together that telling spirits to leave, even with the best of intentions, wasn't necessarily solving the problem.

"Someone says, 'Okay, I'm going to cross this person over.' And they do whatever they do and they believe it, and their intention is for this being to go away," Adam said. "Maybe that energy makes the entity dissipate for a minute or back off a little bit. But prove to me that you're actually sending them somewhere. Where's the proof that that happens?"

He's also seen instances where the activity resumes after a short time. "But we know from evidence that we've captured that when you give an entity resolution and completion, or you've just listened to them, we find that the activity diminishes or it goes away completely."

Chip Coffey makes a specific distinction between spirits

and ghosts. In his view, spirits are entities who have moved on to whatever is next, and who choose to come back from time to time for their own reasons, whether that's to visit loved ones or take care of something they feel isn't totally resolved. "The essence of who we are is our soul," he said, "and our soul at time of death leaves the body. That energy is released. And because free will isn't completely eradicated at time of death, you have a choice to make. Do you, for whatever reason, choose to not complete your transition to spirit or do you make that transition into spirit?" Those that don't make that transition are what he calls ghosts.

I use the terms interchangeably, but I do think he makes an interesting distinction. Chip believes that for the most part, the entities that we communicate with are spirits who we're calling forth to speak to. "Spirits can go anywhere they want to go," he said. "If we were out amongst the crowd and I yelled your name, I'd get your attention."

Ghosts, he believes, are wandering, earthbound entities, and are the ones who are the most troubled. "I've talked to thousands upon thousands of dead people," he said, "and the vast majority of those people who are deceased that I have communicated with are not earthbound and nomadic lost souls." Most of the spirits he speaks to, he explained, have transitioned successfully. "Some of them may be hanging around the earth plane more than others, but most of them have completed their transition into spirit and periodically come back from their dimension in order to communicate with the living."

But even the ones who are adamantly refusing to go, he said, he would never try to force to cross over. "If I feel like somebody is kind of stuck, then I'm going to suggest that when you're ready, you finish your transition," Chip explained. He's not going to flat-out tell anyone what to do, and he certainly doesn't think he has the power to "push" someone into a transition. "I think you can encourage a soul. I think you can pray for that soul. But to say that you're going to cross that person over, and that's that, is a total ego thing. It's just bullshit."

For many reasons, including the fact that we can't assume we know a ghost's personal beliefs, I don't often bring religion into an investigation. But when the nurses at Waverly Hills asked me to pray for them, I did. I will always pray for a ghost who asks. When Adam and I went back to film an episode of *Kindred Spirits* in Season 3, we tried to talk to those nurses again. That part of the sanatorium was closed off because of construction, so we had to stand outside the locked door to the wing. We tried to talk to the nurses, to check back in with them, or at least say hello and tell them we remembered them. But we didn't hear a response.

"That first interaction was so intense and specific," Adam recalled. "They seemed very eager, and involved with what we were doing." We didn't have to hang around for responses from them—they answered right away. "It was almost like this is what they had been waiting for," he said. "This is what we've needed, just for people to listen."

That experience is also why we decided to start investigating larger locations on the show. In the beginning, we wanted to focus only on families, and to try to visit places where we could help both the living and the dead. Eventually, though, we started to think about those nurses, and that there were other locations like Waverly Hills where spirits were still roaming, left behind. No one was paying any attention to them as people at all. Those ghosts could have living family members who have no idea what's happening to them. They're no less deserving of our help.

I think if they wanted to, those nurses could have just come to the other end of the hallway to talk to us when we went back. We don't know if those women didn't hear us, or if they weren't there. I would love to think that after we prayed for them, they felt as though they could move on. What if the knock I heard above my bed that night was one of them telling me that the nurses felt like they were finally free to go? It gives me chills to think about.

MISTAKEN IDENTITY AT
THE MOUNT WASHINGTON HOTEL

The Mount Washington Hotel, in New Hampshire's White Mountains, is one of my favorite places on earth. Charlotte and I have spent many happy vacations there, and Strange Escapes hosts an event there every fall. It's a gorgeous, historic building from the glory days of New Hampshire's grand hotels, when wealthy city dwellers from New York and Boston would head to the country for the summer season to take in the fresh air in turn-of-the-century luxury.

Given that I love that hotel intensely, it will probably not surprise you to learn that it's haunted.

Extremely haunted.

The thing about the Mount Washington, though, is that it doesn't feel scary. If you've been to Disney, you've probably been on the Haunted Mansion ride, where there are "999 happy haunts...but there's room for 1,000." This place feels a lot like that. I've seen shadows at the end of hallways, I've spoken to countless spirits, I've investigated up and down the entire space. But I've never really been scared there. If you ask practically anyone on the staff whether they've ever seen a ghost, they will almost always say yes, but you'll almost never hear from them that it was scary. Trust me: I've asked. A *lot.*

Part of that comes from an openness about the supernatural. The hotel leans into its haunted history. It was built in 1902 by Joseph Stickney, as a wedding gift for his wife, Carolyn Stickney. Joseph, though, died soon after construction had ended. Carolyn, who eventually married a prince and became Princess Carolyn, continued to summer at the hotel for the rest of her life. Now, she's rumored to be the happiest of the happy haunts. Her room—which still has the carved four-poster bed she always traveled with—is the most notoriously haunted of all the haunted places in the hotel. I've spoken to her spirit in the Princess Room, and I've heard ghost stories about that space that would give you goose bumps.

To this day, there's a table in the dining room set for Princess Carolyn, with a sign saying they save a seat for her at dinner every night in the hopes that she'll join them for another meal. And there are portraits of her and Joseph Stickney hanging in the lobby as a tribute to the hotel's founders.

Well, there's a portrait of *a* Joseph Stickney. But not *the* Joseph Stickney.

When the hotel commissioned the paintings, the photo the artist used was of a man named Joseph Stickney. But not the man who built the hotel. The artist mistakenly used the likeness of another man with the same name.

The portrait hanging in the lobby of the Mount Washington? It's of the bank teller who was murdered by Joseph Kelley in Somersworth, New Hampshire, close to the home we investigated with the gravestone in the backyard.

Tell me again my life isn't one long ghost story.

Chapter 5

THERE'S NO SUCH THING AS A GHOST DETECTOR

I WAS ONCE doing an interview with a writer who was clearly open to the supernatural, but who also thought she knew more than she actually did about ghost hunting.

"So when do you use a spectrometer?" she asked.

I stared at her, blank faced. "What's that?"

"Um…isn't that the thing they use to measure ghosts?" she said, on the hot seat. "Like, to see if they're really there?"

"No," I said, laughing. "That's not a thing."[1]

---

1 There actually is such a thing as a spectrometer. It's used to measure light in the electromagnetic spectrum. I've heard people do use it to look for ghosts, I've just never seen it done.

Despite the bumpy start, it all worked out in the end. Years later, she ended up helping me write the book you're reading right now. But that little moment said a lot about what people think happens on an investigation, versus what really does.

As much as I would love real paranormal research to look just like *Ghostbusters*—and as much as people sometimes show up to homes we're investigating and blast that movie's theme song out of their car windows—it's not like that at all. There are no PKE meters to sense psychokinetic energy, no proton packs to stun ghosts, and no traps to grab them and transfer them to containment units.

When I first started investigating, equipment was so key to me, because my initial goal was wanting to prove that ghosts are real. I would go into investigations and constantly stare at my camera, with my recorder rolling the whole time and my K-II meter lighting up. It's very easy to get caught up in all that technical stuff and miss what's happening around you. Over time, I realized the gear is there to support the investigation, not dictate it. It all depends on your personal preference—I've investigated with John Tenney before where the only equipment we used were candles to gauge a spirit's responses—and how comfortable you are with the machines. You could be staring into a viewfinder and miss a full-bodied apparition walking right in front of you.

"The key to being a good investigator is the ability to

strike a healthy balance between being in the moment and unbiased analysis," said Shawn Porter. He's a paranormal investigator who owns GhostStop, a company that manufactures paranormal equipment. "Use the tools effectively to do their job, but don't let it blind you to the process."

He believes that the best analysis happens after the investigation is over. "During the investigation we have a tendency to focus on the acute moment. We're focused on that one room or that one EVP," Shawn said. "We'll walk around staring at the display screens on our cameras and poking at buttons instead of the room in front of us. Take those moments, document them and review them all as a whole once the investigation is done and in the bag. Your senses will have had a chance to stabilize and provide a broader look at all of the larger picture—a collection of the entire investigation."

Besides thinking we're all like *Ghostbusters*, the other assumption people often make is that investigators can just sense ghosts, or that we're all psychic. In reality, it's somewhere between those two things. For me, the best method of investigation is simply sitting, listening, and observing. I do think your energy and intention play significant roles in the outcome of an investigation. If you go into a place scared to death, you'll probably have a scary experience. If you go in to observe and learn, you'll probably have a much less intense, but no less interesting, outcome.

Sometimes, I can sense that the energy is right,

especially in EVP sessions. I can tell when I'm having a good one, even if I can't hear a ghost's responses before I play back the recording. It's almost like I can feel it in the air. And conversely, I can tell when there's nothing going on. That's why I believe the most important part of working on a case is using your intuition, and being in the moment. If you're coming from that place, it's easy to then decide what tools will help you get the best results. (I say this after having done thousands of investigations. In the beginning, of *course* you're going to be obsessed with your equipment. It's really fun to use.)

When we head into a case, the first thing we do when we're choosing to investigate a location is to determine need. Is this a case of living people looking for help, or are there entities in the home that need it? Sometimes, that changes during the investigation itself, but we like to go in with a general idea. Then, I do some high-level research about the house and the area. I compile experiences of people associated with the place—anything that could have led to paranormal activity.

I try to gather as much data as possible before going in, but I also know I'm going to be there for a few nights and the kind of information I'm going to need will evolve as the case unfolds. Multi-night investigations aren't always possible—but we insist on them for the show because we can't fully execute a *Kindred Spirits* investigation without them.

Sometimes, in a perfect world, you can go back time and again over a span of years and a case becomes a case study. One of the most famous examples of an intensive paranormal case study is Harry Price's investigation of the notoriously haunted Borley Rectory in Essex, England. For a time, that house, built in the 1860s, was known as the most haunted house in England. It had a *very* long history of intense hauntings, with people seeing horse-drawn carriages led by headless horsemen and experiencing poltergeist-like activity, such as being thrown from their beds. Price investigated it for a long time, and in 1937, he rented the countryside mansion for a year with the intention of doing a long-term study.

He recruited a team of forty-eight "official observers" to help him investigate for stretches at a time. They were mostly students, and because there were so many of them, Price needed to write a handbook on proper investigation and research techniques. That handbook is credited as the first real guidebook on how to investigate the paranormal. (I wish it were available now, but I haven't been able to find it.) Price wrote many books about his findings from Borley Rectory, which are fascinating on their own and as examples of early paranormal investigation.

To me, the most interesting part is that, during that year, one of the spirits the team contacted said he would burn down the house. Less than a year later, in February 1939, the house did go up in flames. The man who had recently purchased the home claimed to have accidentally knocked a lamp over while unpacking, but the subsequent investigation stated that the fire had been set deliberately. By the ghost? Who knows? The mystery was never solved.[2]

SETTING UP AN INVESTIGATION

The first tool I like to use when we enter a new space is a still camera, but that's before the investigation even begins. I like to document everything in the area, especially where it's laid out. When I'm reviewing evidence later, and I think I'm seeing something strange, it really helps to have some spatial relation of the place—it's easy to forget where things are, and it's helpful to have a frame of reference to go back to.

One key piece of advice from Shawn: Know your equipment before you go to investigate. "Have the tools you are comfortable with, get familiar with them prior to the investigation, then set them to do their job," he said. Setting up gear can take a lot of time away from the actual investigation if you're trying that gear out for the first

2   Adams, P, and E. Brazil (2010). "Borley Rectory." http://www .harrypricewebsite.co.uk/Borley/borley_into.htm. Retrieved 26 June 2020.

time. Another reason: The ghosts don't always operate on your time line. "Events can happen any time," he said. "It's happened while we're setting up, during an interview with the client, or while we're packing the truck. Just like any living person, an intelligent being doesn't have to react because we told them so on the count of three. Would you?"

Personally, after taking photos, I'll do a sweep using an electromagnetic field (EMF) detector. That's to determine whether there are any strong electromagnetic fields in the house that could interfere with electronics. Some people also have reactions to EMF exposure like insomnia, distractedness, or heightened anxiety, which could all affect how they're witnessing what's happening in their house, so it's helpful to know if that's a potential issue.

After that, I'll set up my static cameras. Those keep rolling footage of what's happening in different areas. That is a great resource when I'm investigating in one room and I hear a noise in another—I can go back and review that footage to see if anything showed up on screen.

When I'm ready to start investigating, I like to have my equipment within easy reach if I need it, but not in my hands. I like it to be as natural as possible. I don't want to walk into a room and start talking to these spirits and have all this gear in my hands. It's too distracting. I wouldn't come to your house with a camera in one hand and a recorder in the other and just say, "Hey, my name's

Amy. How's it going? Tell me everything." You'd be like, *What is happening right now?*

In those initial conversations, I tend to investigate just going off the information that the homeowners provide: what they've observed and who they think it might be. On the first night of a case, we generally use only handheld recorders to try to capture electronic voice phenomena, or maybe a structured light sensor (SLS) camera. An SLS camera uses the technology from video games that maps the human body. When it's pointed at an empty space where there are no living people, it can capture entities we can't see, and visually represent them on a screen in the same way it would represent human action on a gaming device. Once, I got SLS footage of someone saluting—so we were able to determine there was a veteran attached to the case, which the homeowner didn't know. The key in the beginning isn't just getting names, it's observing a spirit's actions, then taking that evidence and putting it with actual history and facts, and trying to narrow down who it is.

From there, we'll do more research and sometimes bring in outside experts depending on what evidence we gather on the first night of investigating. We choose which additional pieces of technology to utilize depending on who we think might be there. The thing about tech on the show, and using different methods, is that we're fitting four or five days of investigation into forty-four minutes of airtime. There are lots of different things we try that don't get strong results, so we don't show them. With such a short time to fit the narrative into, we're only going to show you what really worked.

"My primary mission in any piece of equipment we build or use for investigations is to document and enhance our senses," Shawn said. "There are some pieces of equipment that are simply used to enhance and document the environment. There are other devices that take this information and interpret it for the sole purpose of displaying it in a form that we can perceive more easily." Other devices, he explained, might add additional layers to processing that data, but could distort that information. "The bottom line is this: Try anything. Explore and discover. Just be knowledgeable on what you are presenting as evidence."

THE ONE ESSENTIAL PIECE OF TECH: A VOICE RECORDER

One thing I always use, without fail, is a handheld recording device to capture EVPs. Once in a while, you might hear a voice from a spirit with your own ears, but it's almost impossible to have a longer conversation, which actually gives you answers, that way. A voice recorder picks up sounds we can't hear, and plays them back for us. It's also so useful to be able to go back and listen to EVPs more than once to try to decipher what the ghost is saying.

If you own a smartphone, then you already have a voice recorder with you all the time. The microphones and speakers built into those phones do a solid job of recording EVPs, and it's a tool you already own without having to spend anything else.

Adam and I use Panasonic RR-DR60 recorders. If you know anything about paranormal equipment, you know that that model is basically the holy grail for ghost hunters. That's because it isn't manufactured anymore. For a brief time in the 1990s, Panasonic made this noise-activated recorder, which only records when there is a sound, and does an especially good job of capturing the entire thing, and of cutting out the silence. There is no downtime of dead air. You hear noises and that's it. It's a huge time-saver. Other noise-activated recorders, for the most part, will cut off beginnings or ends of words. Not this one.

It took a long time for that particular piece of equipment to catch on in popularity, though. More than a decade ago, I worked with the late Mark and Debby Constantino, who were EVP experts from Nevada. They had a stockpile of the recorders, and they were really the first people to popularize that particular model as being uniquely useful.

Once amateur investigators started seeing RR-DR60s

used on ghost hunting shows, demand for them sky-rocketed. Since then, they've been harder and harder to get—and once they're gone, they're gone. I've even reached out to Panasonic to find out about having them make more of this model, and they weren't interested at all. If you look on the internet right now, you'll probably see them selling for almost two thousand dollars. (I do want to note, though, that you definitely do *not* need one of these to talk to ghosts. I used to get great EVPs with my little handheld Olympus.)

USING K-II EMF METERS IN INVESTIGATIONS

People tend to think that K-II EMF meters are integral to investigations, but that's not always the case for me. I use them, but they're not reliable, because they can be easily interfered with by environmental factors. Even just being near a cell phone can set one off. That's why it's so important to have additional things to consider, like EVPs, to combine with K-II readings.

Once, Adam and I were investigating for *Kindred Spirits* in the National Homestead in Gettysburg, Pennsylvania, which was an orphanage and home for widows after the Civil War. We had a K-II meter and some other sensitive equipment set up on the floor of the basement, which kept going off all at once. They'd light up, then go dark, then light up again, over and over, but those reactions weren't correlating to our investigation. We couldn't figure out what was happening, until I happened to look out the window and saw a police car outside the building. The officer's radio was so strong that every time he made a call, it would make our equipment spike. We already knew not to use our walkies near the equipment because of interference, but I had never seen it happen from outside a building before.

K-II meters can be useful in some circumstances. Sometimes, the lights just attract the attention of ghosts. Another time when we were doing a private investigation in the same orphanage, I lined up some K-IIs on the floor. All of a sudden, a shadow figure ran past them. One by one, the machines went off, as the figure headed toward me. Something grabbed my side and pulled me over. I stumbled, my heart pounding, and I ran over to Adam. "What was that?" I asked him. He didn't know. Everyone in the room saw it all happen, but we didn't capture any evidence explaining what that was. Could it have been hostile? Sure. It's easy to interpret an action like that as having ill intent. But it could have also been the ghost of a little kid who was so happy to see a mom that he got over-excited and ran into me. If you hadn't seen your mother in a lot of years, and you saw someone who reminded you of her, you might have a strong reaction, too. That's why it's so hard to truly know the intention of spirits from a single moment like that—we don't know how hard they have to struggle to communicate, and whether they can fully control their actions. Maybe whatever that was had to expend so much effort to be in the room with us that it just couldn't "hit the brakes," so to speak, quickly enough, and bumped into me accidentally.

(When we went back to the orphanage in Season 3 of *Kindred*, we talked about that experience—and eerily enough, we saw a shadow man in that same spot.)

Sometimes, too, the K-II is the key to solving a case. That's what happened when we investigated the home of Carl and Cindy in Providence, Rhode Island, on Season 2 of *Kindred*. They had been experiencing activity in their home like knocking and footsteps for the five years they owned it, but it had been getting increasingly worse, especially toward Carl. He heard people calling out to him, and once saw a chair lift into the air on its own, flip around, and set itself gently on the ground. Because of the attention directed at him, Carl thought it might be his grandmother Helen. Cindy also had a grandmother who'd passed, named Mary.

As soon as we started investigating, basically as we were putting out equipment, the K-II started going off. I'd ask the ghost to light it up, and it would. In an EVP session, we didn't get a response to the name Helen, but when I asked for Mary, she responded, *Mary is here.* Curiously, though, when we started asking if she were Cindy's grandmother, everything went quiet.

We ended up finding evidence of the previous owner, a man named Jim, who'd died of cancer.

Stephanie, a psychic who came in to help us investigate, told us that he was choosing to stay in his house. Jim just wanted to be left alone to do his own thing, and he would often bump into things, which explained those knocks and steps. "Even though you're not family," she said to Carl and Cindy, "he said it feels like you're family."

But we still couldn't figure out who Mary was. Finally, Carl told us about another family member, his aunt Mary McCartle. Every time we asked if it was her, she would light up the K-IIs.

"Do you have any idea why she'd be around you?" I asked him.

"Oh my God," he said, "she was my godmother."

"She's probably checking in," I guessed. "Even if she's not here all the time, she's probably doing her god-motherly duties."

They were so happy to know that there was no malice to any of the activity, and that there was virtually no chance of the activity escalating to anything dangerous. Their house may have been full of ghosts, but they were ghosts who were choosing to be there for positive reasons. Once they knew what was going on, Carl's and Cindy's sense of relief was palpable.

TRACKING MOVEMENT THROUGH SLS

One of the things I love about paranormal investigation is that you can never tell going in what technique will get the best results. On another case in Season 2 of *Kindred*, we visited a home where really strange things were happening, especially to the kids in the family. Kate and Mike asked us to investigate their home in New Smyrna, Florida. Kate heard voices in the home, and she had her hair pulled by unseen forces. Her son Gavin was so scared he started sleeping on the floor in his sister Hailey's bedroom. He didn't like to hear the washing machine go on by itself in the middle of the night. Hailey woke up to a shadow figure standing over her bed. Kate and Mike were so afraid of the impact on their four kids that they tried to sell their home.

Mike personally felt as though he dodged an attack in the house. When he tried to open up an attic door in the ceiling that had been sealed shut with paint, a box cutter flew out at him. "It was almost like a booby trap," he said. "The way it came out, it was like it was meant to hurt somebody."

On the first night of investigation, I used the SLS camera in the master bedroom, where Kate had experienced a lot of activity. Almost immediately, I saw a form on the screen. I asked it to wave, and it waved right back at me.

Just then, a larger form appeared on the screen. It looked as though it grabbed the hand of the smaller figure, and all of a sudden, they both disappeared.

That's a huge piece of evidence to capture, especially on the first night. The way they interacted with each other made me think they were connected in some way. On the second night, though, we couldn't get anything. Not a single EVP, except for one very faint *yes* when we asked if we were talking to Gavin's godfather, Mike, who had passed away.

In research the next day, I found previous owners of the home, Edna and Paul Cowell. Edna had been convinced that the house was killing her. Her home was constructed in a place that was not zoned for building because of poor drainage in the land. As a result, it was filled with mold and mildew. She fought the city for help in fixing the problem, saying that the condition of the home was causing lung damage. The property records included all her handwritten notes, plus records of city council meetings where she pleaded for assistance. Ultimately, Edna died of chronic obstructive pulmonary disease (COPD), which she believed was caused by the toxic atmosphere in the house.

Immediately, it clicked. The attic had been sealed off to encapsulate the mold inside. Edna and Paul were trying to warn them that the house was a danger to their family. With that, we were able to finally speak to Edna.

"What was wrong with the house?" I asked her.

Mold, she said.

"We're wondering if when they tried to open the attic, it upset you."

Yes.

It turns out, she was right. We brought in a mold specialist who found fungal growth in the baby's bedroom. Luckily, it was minimal enough that they could address the problem before anyone got sick. We told Edna that she had helped to warn the family and that they would be safe because of her.

We also uncovered more evidence that Gavin's god-father was also present, looking over his godson, probably trying to protect him from the unseen dangers in the house. "I love it that he's here," Mike said. "That's comforting."

Since they took care of the mold in the house, the family hasn't reported any activity from Paul and Edna.

SCANNING FOR VOICES WITH A SPIRIT BOX

One technique that tends to have really strong results for us is the spirit box. This tool scans radio waves to create white noise that people believe a spirit can manipulate to communicate and make their words heard. The spirit box technology we use now grew out of what was called a Frank's Box, invented in 2002 by Frank Sumption. In that early version, Sumption modified radios so that they flipped through stations at different rates of speed. Frank's Box, though, was built to communicate with aliens—he even claims to have gotten the instructions to build the boxes from the aliens themselves.

"His predecessor was a Latvian inventor by the name of Konstantin Raudive," said Greg Newkirk, who, with his wife Dana, runs the Traveling Museum of the Paranormal & Occult. They often bring it to Strange Escapes events. "He started to believe that with what eventually became known as the Raudive diode circuit, he could pull the voices of the dead out of the air." One of Raudive's books, *Breakthrough*, published in 1971, came with a vinyl record of EVPs. You can still listen to recordings of it on the internet pretty easily. "While there are earlier examples of accidental EVP recordings, that was arguably the beginning of instrumental transdimensional communication," Greg added. "Then people like Frank came along and tried to build upon a lot of that."

I was one of them. I even made my own Frank's Box back in the day, before modern spirit boxes were being manufactured, using instructions I found on the internet. There was this little radio you could buy at RadioShack that was easy to open up and modify.

The spirit box can be incredibly useful, but there's a possibility of bias in the evidence you gather from it. Because we're asking questions and then listening for the answers, it's entirely possible we could be hearing answers we *want* to hear rather than what's actually being said. Unlike EVPs on a recording device, we can't play back what comes out of the spirit box. We hear it once, and it's gone.

That's why we were so intrigued when we saw a video of Karl Pfeiffer and Connor Randall using the spirit box for a different kind of communication. It was a technique called the Estes Method that they developed with another investigator, Michelle Tate, when they were resident investigators in 2016 at the Stanley Hotel (in Estes Park, Colorado—hence the name).

In that method, one person asks questions, and one person listens to the spirit box for answers. The person listening, though, is wearing a blindfold and noise-canceling headphones, to eliminate as much outside influence as possible. "The idea was to basically isolate someone and see if the responses still lined up without any of that human bias or expectation influencing the answers," Karl said. The idea, they explained, was to try to eliminate group bias from the investigation.

"I think anybody going on investigations regularly sees it happen. Somebody hears an EVP or something that they think is a voice and they say, *Oh, it's saying this.* And then suddenly that's in everybody's mind," Connor said. "That's the largest issue with spirit boxes. People are playing these random radio frequency generators and of course they're spitting out sounds because they're sounds on the radio. But if somebody in the group suggests something, suddenly that becomes the answer."

In this method, if you're the receiver, you can't hear any of the questions being asked, so it's unlikely your answers will be skewed toward what you *want* to hear versus what you're actually hearing. With your other senses blocked out and your focus completely on the white noise coming from the spirit box, you almost go into a little bit of a trance when you're listening for answers. The more we've done it, the more we've questioned whether we're really hearing voices from the spirit box itself, or we're just putting ourselves into a state where we're able to hear the voices in our heads.

"Having somebody so focused on that noise can put them in something like a trance state," Connor said. "At that point, you're wondering if it's a ghost speaking, or it's a psychic middle place that enables something to occur. We're not sure where the answers are coming from, but people will go into a different state of mind when they go in there, and as of now it seems to be working to communicate with something quite often."

Greg Newkirk agrees with Connor. "I think there's an element to these types of devices that puts people in a trance state, because their conscious mind is busy listening to this radio circuit, so their subconscious mind is able to slip into psychic impressions a lot easier," he said. "I think that our consciousness is a lot more complex than we give it credit for. And I think that's where a lot of this stuff is happening. Sometimes you just need, essentially, a white noise generator to calm your mind to the point where you can start to pick up on that stuff."

There are so many interesting variations on this method that people are still developing, like doing long-distance questioning through a baby monitor, or having multiple people who are isolated from each other act as receivers. Greg and Dana, with Karl and Connor, did some fascinating experiments that combined spirit boxes with other, lesser-known methodologies in their documentary series *Hellier*, which is a deep dive into one paranormal case that ends up connecting to aliens and ancient gods. In one episode, they combine the Estes Method with a piece of equipment called the "god helmet," which is believed to put the brain in the same state it's in during a religious, psychic, or supernatural experience. In the experiment, Dana wears the helmet and, in her amplified psychic state, asks questions to Connor—blindfolded and wearing noise-canceling headphones—acting as the receiver. The ensuing conversation, they think, is with an extraterrestrial being.

Right? It's so cool.

On *Kindred Spirits*, we've been experimenting with limited knowledge to see if that affects results with the Estes Method. Sometimes, when Adam is acting as the receiver, I'll pull out information that he doesn't know yet, and use it in my questions. In that method, I know there's no way his answers are influenced in some way by his current knowledge of the case. That's something we've started doing pretty regularly—instead of filling him in on research that I've done, we'll do an Estes Method session, and the results become even more interesting.

One of the most intense experiences I've ever had with a spirit box happened in Season 4 of the show, when we visited the Farrar School in Maxwell, Iowa. Built in 1922, it's a famously haunted (now closed) elementary school, which the owners, Jim and Nancy, purchased with the intention of turning it into an events space. In the year and a half before we went there, they felt as though something very dark had come into play. There were multiple reports of a shadow man popping up throughout the building and terrorizing the people inside.

On the first night of our investigation, we used the Estes Method to try to get a read on the situation. Adam asked questions, and I received answers like *I died, The farm, April, I was cut, Make it right.*

The next day, we did some investigating at the local library, and found the town's only unsolved murder. In

1975, the body of a man named Terry had been found with his throat cut. He had been there several months when he was discovered. When? In April.

With that information, we went back to the school—but the more we investigated, the more we realized there were additional spirits in the space, and Terry was negatively affecting them. Signs increasingly pointed to Terry being the menacing shadow man, to the point where he was even harassing the other ghosts. In an EVP session, I asked, "Is there someone here you don't trust?" The answer: *Terry.*

However, there were so many ghosts that we were having a hard time speaking to one of them at a time, and Terry, the one we really needed to talk to, was hiding behind the others and reluctant to communicate. So we asked Chip Coffey for his help in a method of investigation we had never tried on the show before. He and I sat side by side, both blindfolded and wearing headphones, listening to separate spirit boxes. Our hope was that if the other spirits were making contact with Chip, I would be able to make direct contact with Terry.

I did. And he wasn't happy.

"Terry doesn't have to talk about it," Adam said, "but somebody else could just tell me if Terry's here."

Do your job, I heard. *Fuck you guys.*

At that point, he was pretty sure that Terry was speaking to me, and the other sprits were talking to Chip.

"Why are you here, Terry?" Adam asked. "Do you need our help at all?"

All right, let's get to it, I heard.

"The activity that you're doing is affecting everybody here," he said. I heard someone laughing in my headphones. "I know something bad happened to you. We can't fix that. But do you want to talk about it?"

Terry kept dodging the questions, while next to me, Chip was channeling messages with increasing urgency and fear. *He's coming,* Chip heard. *It's him. Hide.*

While that was happening, something kept shoving my chair.

"You need to leave Amy alone, Terry," Adam said.

Get bent, I heard.

At that point, Adam switched with me, believing that Terry was toying with me and that he might get better responses because Terry wasn't as interested in him.

"What do you need to say, Terry?" I asked.

I'm getting stronger, Adam heard. *I like it here.*

"I like it here too," I said, "but you have to treat people with respect. Can you do that?"

Older brother, he heard.

"One of your brothers has passed. Did you know that? If you moved on you could be with him."

I didn't know.

"You didn't know your brother had passed? Your mom passed as well."

You stop.

"You're here, but you could be with them. Do you know that?"

I'm frightened.

"You're allowed to be frightened," I said, "but you really don't have to stay here. What do you want us to do for you?"

Go away.

"This is tough for you, I know," I said.

I'm not into God. Deliverance.

"Is that what you're afraid of? Is that why you're not moving on? Are you afraid where you'll go? Do you want to keep talking? If you go…"

You're the problem.

"If you stay here, can you please stop bullying the other people here? Can you behave?"

I belong.

"You do," I responded, "but you need to be fair to the other people who were here before you. Can you do that? You can be a part of this or you can move on and be with your family, but either way you have to behave."

Honest as possible.

It seemed to us like he was afraid to move on because of what might happen to him, and that he wanted to stay in the school. "He feels like the odd man out, and he's confused about how to behave here," Chip explained. We thought it was possible that his hostile behavior was really defensive behavior, and that's why he was being so forceful with the other spirits and living people in the space. Acknowledging him, we hoped, was going to get him to calm down.

Our speculation is that Terry came to the school because it had been investigated more since the new owners purchased the building. Adam and I have a theory that when people investigate a spot frequently, it attracts more ghosts, because that spot becomes like a beacon for them. Terry may have been one of those drawn in.

To help him feel welcomed, and to encourage him to be more at peace, we put up a little memorial on a chalkboard in one of the classrooms. People who visit can write messages to Terry, and let him know that he's remembered. We've heard that it's helped a lot, and that he's just one of the regular ghosts now, getting along with everyone else. It didn't make it into the show, but our theory is that until the murder is solved, he's going to stick around. It's going to take a lot for him to decide to move on.

COMMUNICATING WITH KIDS THROUGH A BOO BUDDY

One of Shawn Porter's most innovative developments is the Boo Buddy, a piece of investigative equipment built inside a teddy bear. People sometimes question why that's necessary, but just like living kids, the spirits of children can be shy and afraid to talk to strangers. The Boo Buddy is so convincing as a toy that my own daughter some-times steals it to play with. There was one case where that bear was the key to figuring out what was happening in a home.

On Season 1 of *Kindred*, Adam and I went to a home outside Pittsburgh, Pennsylvania, where Kristy and her two young kids reported seeing a looming shadow figure in their home. She thought it might be her grandmother, who'd died in her bedroom. Kristy had bought her grand-mother's house, even though the two had a falling out years before the older woman passed away. We did find evidence, with Chip Coffey's help, that the grandmother was there, and that she was sending messages of love to Kristy and her family.

But Chip also picked up on another story, a much darker one he felt was tied to abuse. In an Estes Method session, Adam asked for the spirit's name, and I heard, *Amy*. He followed up, asking "Do you know *this* is Amy?" *I don't.*

We did some research of the area, and we found one of the most terrible stories I've ever encountered. In a house not too far away from Kristy's, there had been a little girl named Amy in the mid-1980s. She was three and a half years old when her stepmother forced her into a scalding hot bath. Amy begged to get out of the 138°F water, but the woman forced her to stay in. The little girl got first- and third-degree burns over most of her body, and she died of cardiac arrest in the hospital early the next morning.

I just can't imagine anything more terrible than that.

We had to try to reach her.

Because we thought it was likely we were making contact with Amy, we used a Boo Buddy the next night. Inside the teddy bear, there are sensors that can pick up touch, EMFs, EVPs, and temperature changes. When something touches it, the bear says, "That tickles!" And when the temperature goes up or down, the bear asks if it was the spirit making that change.

Adam, Chip, and I sat around the bear, hoping we'd be able to speak to Amy. As I was recounting the story to Chip of what had happened to her, all of a sudden we heard: "Did you make it warm in here?"

"We were talking about hot water," Chip said, "and the temperature went up."

With that, we felt strongly that she was in the room with us. "There's a lot of love in this room," Chip said, talking to her, "and you don't have to be afraid to be here with us."

"Amy," I asked. "Are you okay? If you're okay, can you light up these lights for us?" The K-II meter lit up.

"Do you like being here because there are other kids to play with?" Adam asked. Again, the lights.

"If you want to stay and play, you can do that, too. But there's nothing to be afraid of anymore," I told her, heartbroken that this little girl who had been hurt for no reason had been staying behind for so long. "No one's going to hurt you ever again. But you don't need to stay in this place."

With that, the activity stopped. Something changed in the room. We all felt that Amy had left.

These few basics are really just the tip of the iceberg when it comes to equipment for research and investigating. Paranormal investigative equipment is constantly evolving, because investigators are always tinkering with existing products to better fit the needs for their particular experiments. It's so exciting to see what's born out of this intense interest in the field.

A HAUNTING IN THE BATHROOM

After college, I was living with my boyfriend in Placerville, California. I had just had my wisdom teeth out, so I was taking antibiotics. One night, I went upstairs to brush my teeth and take my evening pills, and the bottle was nowhere to be found.

"Have you seen my pills?" I asked.

"They're right on the counter," my boyfriend answered.

The sink area was completely empty except for our toothbrushes. "They're not there," I said. So he went up to look, and he couldn't find them anywhere.

I went back into the bathroom, just to check again, but nothing. At that point, I was having a little bit of a meltdown. I was raised in a house where things moved, and I had just had it. "Listen," I said to the empty room. "I don't know why you took those pills. It's medicine. I need it. I have an infection and it's helping me. So can you please put it back?"

As I turned to leave, I shut off the light. But then, I stopped in my tracks. Something in my head said, *Turn the light on, and turn around.*

The pills were right there, in the middle of the counter. Two of us had checked, and we never could have missed them in that spot.

Something had put them back while the light was off.

Chapter 6

IT'S NOT ALWAYS A GHOST

IF YOU THINK your house has a ghost, I have some bad news for you.

It's probably not actually haunted.

I know. It's disappointing to me, too. But when people tell me their house is haunted, I go through a mental laundry list of all the things it could be that aren't supernatural. There could be mechanical problems with the house, or people could be experiencing physical or mental health issues that present the same way as para-normal phenomena. Believe it or not, a lot of this job is proving that things *aren't* ghosts.

That was one of the great things about being on *Ghost Hunters*, especially in the beginning. The show was very big on skepticism, and it was all about debunking. We didn't go into a space with the mindset that we would definitely find a ghost—we went in trying to find other reasons to explain why things were happening. Everybody was so hard on evidence and experiences, and they were so thorough with walk-throughs to find any external factors that were potential complications. I felt right at home in that aspect. Not only did the team encourage it, but the production company encouraged it, and the network encouraged it.

Steve Gonsalves, one of my costars on the show, always said that the harder you are on the evidence, it makes the evidence that much stronger when you can't disprove it. To me, it's just as impressive to find a "real" solution to something as it is to find something paranormal. You're solving the problem, just in a different way. And that kind of solution is equally as important, because the more we find these false positives and learn to look for them, the easier it is down the road to give something the smell test, eliminate it, and focus on the more puzzling activity.

Having a healthy dose of skepticism is essential to succeeding as a paranormal researcher. Once you've been at it awhile, you'll see commonalities between people's claims, and be able to find explanations for them more easily. But you'll also see how quickly people want you to say that it's a ghost before a rational explanation. So that skepticism is essential, because you're going in with the intention of trying to find the more practical issue or explanation so that people won't be afraid of their own homes.

And a lot of times, honestly, it is strictly a physical issue with your house. Weird noises are undeniably creepy, and doors slamming shut on their own have never made anyone comfortable. But there are definitely cases where your home itself is scaring you, rather than a supernatural problem inside it.

Problems coming from the home itself are generally pretty easy to identify. The biggest one is noisy pipes. Doors slam shut on their own if windows are open, even in other rooms, because airflow can create a vacuum that pulls the door closed. Maybe the house is a little bit uneven, or the floors are crooked, and that explains doors swinging on their own. Maybe the door casings are off and the door just naturally slingshots. Maybe you're waking up with odd hallucinations because the alarm clock next to your bed, which is twenty years old, is giving off a high EMF field and messing with your brain.

Some investigators like to use thermal-imaging cameras to try to see entities that are different temperatures in a space, but I find them particularly useful to find things in the walls, like animal infestations, that can explain odd noises. Adam and I once went on a case for *Ghost Hunters* where we were trying to explain creepy happenings in an apartment above a restaurant in New Jersey. We had to sleep there overnight, and in the middle of the night, I heard scratching noises. I grabbed the thermal-imaging camera and spotted an animal inside the wall.

The same thing happened before I was on television, when I was helping to investigate a restaurant in Southern California. A restaurant had what they thought was a haunting. They would come in every day and find glasses shattered on the ground, and they had no idea why it was happening. The team set up a DVR camera over-night, and captured a rat scaling the wall and climbing behind the glasses and knocking them over. The restau-rant had no idea (or, at least, they didn't tell us) they had rats.

When I meet people who are interested in ghosts, one of the most common things they'll ask is for me to look at a photo that they're sure has a supernatural presence in it. They're hoping I'll verify their theory and say there's something weird happening in the shot. I always tell people not to show me their pictures of ghosts unless they want to find out those photos aren't actually of ghosts. It's too easy to mistake dust, or shadows, or reflections for something more interesting.

Photo debunking is one of my least favorite parts of paranormal investigation. Because I wasn't there when the photo was taken, I can't verify what was really going on, and I can't just vouch for what people say and take that as fact. There are too many instances where people will claim the out-of-focus woman in the background of a shot was "definitely not there," when in reality she shows up in another photo from the same event and the people in the first shot just didn't notice her.

That happens a lot on ghost tours, especially at haunted places like Gettysburg, Pennsylvania, or Williamsburg, Virginia. People are looking for ghosts around every corner, and they're so ready to think that the shadow in the back of their photo is really a person. Did you really do an inventory of everyone in your twenty-person group, and their precise locations at the moment this photo was taken, such that you are sure beyond a doubt no one was there?

There are two common psychological phenomena at play when it comes to "haunted" photos, as well as for other instances where you're convinced something supernatural is happening. One is pareidolia, which is the tendency to see patterns and images in places like clouds or in abstract patterns. Human brains are optimized to recognize faces, so we tend to see them when they're not actually there. It's related to apophenia, a term originated by German psychiatrist Klaus Conrad, in 1958. In a paper about the early stages of schizophrenia, Conrad defined it as the tendency to perceive connections between things that aren't connected or related in any way.

This is especially common with what people believe are

religious images showing up in food. In 2004, a Florida woman sold a grilled cheese that she believed had the image of the Virgin Mary on it to a casino for $28,000. That story spawned massive media attention—even inspiring an episode of the TV show *Glee* called "Grilled Cheesus"—but it's far from the only one. People claim the "NunBun" in Nashville, Tennessee, has an image of Mother Teresa, and a "miracle tortilla" in New Mexico and a burnt fish stick in Ontario, Canada, have images of Jesus. Twice—once in India and once in England—women claim to have cut open an eggplant to discover the word "Allah" spelled out in its seeds.

So if you see something in a photo that's not really there, you're not crazy. (At least, you're probably not crazy. I'm not a doctor. Don't quote me.) Your brain is looking for it, and your openness to the weirdness in the world is telling you it's something supernatural.

While pareidolia shows people what isn't actually there, there's another psychological phenomenon that doesn't show you what *is* actually there. That's called selective attention. In this instance, it's the tendency of the human brain to only focus on one part of what's happening, at the exclusion of other equally significant things occurring at the same time. For an example of this, look up "The Monkey Business Illusion," a famous video by Harvard researchers Christopher Chabris and Daniel Simons. In that video, there are six people playing basketball: Three in white shirts, and three in black shirts. The video prompts you to count how many times the people in white shirts pass the ball back and forth. While you're concentrating on that, a person in a gorilla suit walks through the frame, beats its chest with its fists, and walks out of the frame again.

Once the action is over, the video goes on to explain that about half the people watching it for the first time (if they haven't heard of an experiment like this before) miss the gorilla, because they're concentrating so intently on the basketball. But then, it gets even better. The video goes on to explain that even if you *have* heard of this experiment, and therefore know to look out for the gorilla, you may not have noticed that the background of the video changes color, or that one of the players in black walks off screen.

Selective attention is a big issue in paranormal investigation, because people are looking for what they want to see, sometimes at the expense of what's actually happening. That's one of the reasons I'm less interested in investigative technology these days. Just like in real life, the more engaged you are with a screen, the less you notice what's going on around you.

I'll be the first to admit that it's disappointing when a photo doesn't turn out to be what you had hoped it would be. You have to come to terms with that as an investigator, and be ready to consider possibilities that aren't the answer you wanted. More than that, you have to be able to admit when you were wrong. It happens a lot when people have a piece of evidence they're excited about, and they'll ask another researcher for an opinion, and that person provides what is a more rational explanation for what's going on in the photo. The person with the photo will often become defensive and upset, rather than trying to be open-minded and learning from the situation. That's why, when people ask me to look at their photos, even though I sound like a jerk when I say it, I respond that they shouldn't give it to me unless they really are open to the idea that they're not going to get the answer they want.

The common things that create weird images in photos are bugs, moisture, or smudges on the lens, mist or smoke in the air, a hair or a strap hanging in front of the camera, or spiderwebs. There are vast resources on the internet showing you examples of what each thing looks like as photo interference. When you think you've captured something paranormal, you might want to check those first to make sure you really have something worth closer examination.

Orb photos, especially, are problematic to me. I've experienced light anomalies that present as a sphere and emit light. I've seen them with my own eyes, and I've captured them on camera. The problem is, they looked nothing like an orb that you get in a photo. What you think is an orb in a photo is almost always carpet fibers or dust, or tiny spiders crawling across the lens. We see them all the time with our DVR cameras. With the advent of digital photography and the enhanced depth of field it can capture, orbs show up more than ever, and they are almost never what you think they are.

One of the other common reasons people assume they have something paranormal happening in their home is that, to some, a ghost is an easier explanation than a health issue with themselves or one of their loved ones.

I get a lot of emails from people who say that a child is experiencing something paranormal, like their daughter is seeing a shadow man in her closet, is too scared to sleep at night, and won't go into her bedroom anymore. They will say it's a huge problem, and they need to get rid of the shadow man as soon as possible. My response is always the same: "What does your pediatrician say?" A lot of the time, the answer is indignant. They'll be upset I consider other possibilities rather than accepting immediately that their child is haunted. I never understand that response. Kids see things all the time. Wouldn't you want it to be normal, childlike behavior rather than an actual ghost harassing your kid all night?

There is a huge spectrum of physical issues that could be mistaken for supernatural phenomena. Sleep paralysis and sleep hallucinations are huge ones. With those conditions, people wake up totally unable to move, or they hallucinate terrifying things happening to them. It is *very* easy to assume there's something menacing in the room that's causing that situation. I know that because I personally have had sleep paralysis and hallucinations. There are times when I wake up, totally unable to move, and I see huge spiders crawling across the pillow toward my face. When you haven't had that situation explained to you, of *course* you're going to assume it's paranormal. It's absolutely terrifying to have that happen, especially when you're half asleep and not in a fully lucid state. I've also heard reports that people coming out of comas, or coming off ventilators, report seeing and hearing things that seem beyond the normal realm. Carbon monoxide and mold have also been known to cause hallucinations.

Sarah Coombs is a psychotherapist who studies the intersection of the paranormal and mental illness. "There's a whole list of diagnoses that include auditory, visual, and even tactile hallucinations, that could easily be mistaken for paranormal activity," she said. When investigating a home, especially when there are inter-personal family dynamics at play, she believes that there are times it makes sense to consider mental health issues as a possibility. "To be sure that it's truly paranormal, which means we can't find any other explanation for it, you'd almost be remiss not to rule out a mental health disorder first."

I've seen a lot of cases where I suspect that what's going on in a home has more to do with the living people in it more than it has to do with a supernatural presence. I especially see this when parents try to tell me their kids are haunted, or possessed, and they say they have to pursue spiritual intervention—but they refuse to consider the idea of medical intervention. When I suggest calling a doctor, there have been times when people have been furious with me, acting so defensive that they try to publicly berate me for suggesting it might be a good idea to get a medical opinion. "It's a self-serving cognitive bias," Sarah said. Those people want to believe they're haunted rather than admit there could be a problem that can't be solved with something as simple as a paranormal investigation.

To be crystal clear: I'm not suggesting that if you think there's a presence in your house, that is a cause for concern over your mental or physical health. I'm talking about a very narrow and specific set of circumstances where I've investigated a home, and the evidence I've found doesn't correlate with what's happening within the family, or when what someone is describing sounds more like a health issue than a haunting. I'm also not suggesting that if you have a mental health concern, there's anything wrong with that, either. The stigma around mental health is unnecessary and unfair. I am simply trying to advocate for situations in which it could be beneficial to you or your family to consult a medical professional or mental health expert.

A lot of times, too, a health issue is only part of the problem. Paranormal situations bring on stress, so it's common for someone who has underlying health concerns to be in a heightened state from that increased tension and difficulty in the home. There are definitely situations where explaining the paranormal activity only illuminates part of what's happening. Out of respect for that person's privacy, we very rarely air that part of the conversation on *Kindred Spirits*, but it happens more often than you might think.

There are many transitory and/or treatable conditions that can have visual or auditory hallucinations, such as severe major depressive disorder. "Almost everyone will be depressed at some point in their lives," Sarah said. "If it is severe enough, it can affect the brain's neurotransmitter levels and trigger psychotic features including hallucinations and delusions. We still don't know exactly why this occurs—one hypothesis is that a disruption in your serotonin and dopamine receptors, which are both key in regulating mood, can induce hallucinatory effects." This holds true for the long-term, chronic mood disorders as well such as bipolar disorder, schizophrenia, and schizoaffective disorder, she added, all of which often have hallucinatory and delusional symptoms when left untreated. Substance use and addiction withdrawal can also alter brain chemistry in similar ways, albeit as a direct effect of an ingested, recreational drug.

Another consideration to keep in mind is the role that traumatic events can play on our perceptions, and acceptance, of our experience of the world. "Trauma, especially childhood trauma and the resultant PTSD that follows, can produce long-lasting emotional issues, including for the family members of the person who has directly experienced the trauma," she said. The stories she's heard from people making claims of a supernatural presence terrorizing a family most often occur when that family is also dealing with traumatic events that have caused lasting, unspeakable pain. "That's a very hard thing to accept, and it's much easier to say there's something else that's doing this to us," Sarah explained. A haunting is something you can't be blamed for, and something you don't have control over. Opening yourself up to the vulnerability, the shame, and the guilt that often accompany events such as physical/sexual abuse and/or domestic violence—whether inflicted on you or someone you love—is incredibly difficult, and it can take years of hard, highly emotional work in therapy to overcome.

Grief and bereavement can have the same effect. "It's not depression in the classic sense, but the processing of grief can often put you in a depressive state that is very acute, severe, and painful, which may also result in hallucinations," she explained. "Usually it's specific to the loved one they have lost, and those tend to go away in time. It's still considered to be within the realm of normal grief processing. However, and this might be my own cognitive bias as a believer in the afterlife, I also think it's possible that you are tapping into whatever impression or essence is left of that person—that a window of time exists where they can still possibly communicate with you. As such, I never discount a bereaved client's experience as a purely hallucinatory effect.

"I do not want to give the impression that all paranormal phenomena can be written off with a mental health diagnosis," Sarah added. "I am unquestionably a believer in the paranormal. But I also think 99 percent of what people report can be chalked up to much more mundane explanations." Like me, Sarah believes that sifting through what isn't supernatural makes finding that 1 percent where it truly is beyond the veil all the more meaningful.

Even in cases where there isn't a health factor at play, there have been times when the homeowners didn't want to hear the results Adam and I had for them after our investigation.

Remember how I was saying that the majority of cases feel as though they have resolution? There have definitely been a few times when the homeowners felt as though they didn't get what they were looking for.

Usually, that happens when the results of the

investigation aren't as exciting as people want them to be. Nobody calls in a ghost hunter and expects to hear that there's an issue with their plumbing. If you ask for a paranormal investigation, it's because you really think there could be something happening in your space. I understand it's disappointing when this turns out not to be the case. But I've set up my entire life around the study of ghosts because of how much I believe in them, so if I'm sitting there telling you I couldn't find a ghost in your house, there's probably not a ghost in your house.

People don't want to hear that, though. They get indignant or angry, because they want to hear the explanation they're expecting to hear, and they don't take the evidence and our findings seriously. What they're experiencing is actually confirmation bias, and it's one of the biggest problems that people in the field face while we're investigating. People want the thing they're experiencing to be a ghost so badly that they invent something that isn't there. From the outside, it's plain to see the evidence doesn't lead to a conclusion that there's paranormal activity, but sometimes people want it to be a ghost so desperately they'll say anything to make a case that you're wrong. I've had people try to discredit me because I didn't find a ghost in their home, or because they believe the shadow in their photo is a ghost and not, say, a statue in the garden. In situations like this, you could give them a thousand rational explanations, but they're going to cling to the ghostly one even though it makes all of us paranormal investigators look bad. Of *course* we want to find ghosts. But we would not be credible in the field unless we took an extremely critical eye to our work.

This is where Kris Williams's skepticism was incredibly helpful. She was always watching out for confirmation bias, and was hypervigilant in making sure there was no other possible explanation for what we were seeing other than the paranormal. I noticed a shift in the mindset of the audience over my time on the show, though. In the beginning, people would ask us if we had eliminated every possibility. They'd ask if we checked the windows, the doors, the wind in the room. But by the time I left the show, people didn't want to hear those explanations. When I would say that the wind made a door slam, they'd respond that it was *definitely* a demon or a ghost, and that there was *no possible way* it wasn't. They'd tell me that I didn't know what I was talking about—when I was there, and they were the ones watching me from home as I performed the investigation.

Another factor at play in these instances is that, theoretically, in certain circumstances, we can actually create ghosts. In 1972 a group of researchers in Canada conducted a famous trial called the Philip experiment, where they wrote a history and a backstory for a ghost, and basically willed it into existence. "They drew pictures of him, and then they tried to contact him," John Tenney explained. "Slowly, over the months, they came into contact with the person they had created, Philip Aylesford." They invented the idea of this person and then started getting activity that mimicked their perception of this ghost they'd made up.[3]

It might seem like a crazy idea that you can invent a ghost, but it's definitely possible. There are cases like the Philip experiment, where it has happened intentionally, and cases I've investigated where it's happening unintentionally. That idea, John explained, dates back to a researcher named T. C. Lethbridge whose theory was that a person's psychic shock from having a traumatic event, or witnessing one, could leave a feeling in a room. "When someone else goes in there, they experience that original person's feeling of panic or dread, and they add to it," he said. "Collectively over the years, that energy starts to form an identity. As people go in and try to give it names, or try to talk to it like it's a person, the thing in the location takes on the identity of what it's being told it is.

"There's no original ghost, but the place ends up becoming haunted by the people who are investigating the location for a ghost," he added.

That thing is called an aggregor. I've encountered one on

3   Wehrstein, K. (2018). "Philip Psychokinesis Experiments." *Psi Encyclopedia.* London: The Society for Psychical Research. https://psi-encyclopedia.spr.ac.uk/articles/philip-psychokinesis-experiments. Retrieved 26 June 2020.

the *Queen Mary*, a former cruise ship that is now a hotel in Long Beach, California. The ship, sometimes called "the Grey Ghost," was launched in 1934 and served as an Atlantic ocean liner until 1967. It has a long and very creepy history. During World War II, the British passenger ship was conscripted as a transport vessel for soldiers. In 1942, while it was bringing fifteen thousand soldiers from New York to Scotland, what was then the RMS *Queen Mary* collided with the HMS *Curacoa*, its escort ship, off the coast of Ireland. It sliced the smaller ship in half, and more than three hundred people aboard the *Curacoa* drowned.

There are a lot of other gruesome deaths attributed to the ocean liner's history—at least forty-nine, to be specific—and many of them are hard to verify. There are stories of a girl drowning in the ship's swimming pool, and of a worker in the boiler room who was cut in half when a heavy door closed on him. One particularly chilling tale involves a man who was arrested on board, and locked alone inside a stateroom by the authorities, only to be found completely eviscerated in a way that he could have never done to himself.

So you probably won't be surprised that the boat, which permanently docked as a floating hotel and museum in the port of Long Beach, has a lot of ghosts roaming its corridors. I've seen many of them. The last time I stayed there, the lamp kept going on and off in my room in what seemed like a very deliberate way.

But curiously, there is something supernatural on the ship that *isn't* a ghost.

After it was retired as an ocean liner, the ship was purchased by Disney, which wanted to develop a theme park at sea. The Imagineers used one room, B340, as the prototype for a stateroom that was like the Haunted Mansion. They wired the room so that floorboards would creak when no one was walking on them, faucets would turn on and off on their own, and spooky faces would appear behind the mirror.

If you know how much I love Disney, you can only imagine how much I wish that had actually happened. But the plan turned out to be unprofitable, and was shut down. The room, though, still had Disney's intellectual property inside, so it was locked for many years. Because the room was always "mysteriously" locked, and because people knew the ship's history and its reputation for unexplained phenomena, B340 became known as the haunted room. People would go looking for ghosts on board, and they'd always go to B340. People were constantly looking for ghosts in room B340, they were attributing negative energy to the space, and things started to form in the room.

The last time we held a Strange Escapes event on the *Queen Mary*, Greg and Dana Newkirk and John Tenney were holding investigations in that room. In small groups throughout the night, people would investigate the space, asking questions into the dark and hoping for answers. Greg and Dana brought some of their haunted objects from the Traveling Museum of the Paranormal & Occult, and Dana used tarot cards during their investigations to read the energy in the room and help guide the line of questioning. They were getting responses, but those responses weren't really coherent in any way. The only through line was frustration and anger in the responses. Every time they asked its name, they would get nothing. It was one of the only questions that got no response at all.

"Why won't you tell us your name?" Greg asked. "If you don't have a name, now might be a good time to give yourself one."

Hassle, was the only response.

They realized they were most likely dealing with an aggregor, which was forming out of all the negativity people were ascribing to the room. It didn't say its name because it didn't actually *have* a name. And, apparently, couldn't be bothered to choose one. When you have a space like this, which has become so notorious for being haunted, people go in with a hyperawareness of the potential for something to happen. The hotel has ramped up the amount of ghost tours and spooky experiences you can have there, and has embraced B340's haunted history, even going so far as to put up spooky photos inside the room and emblazon the walls with ghost stories and sightings people have shared on the ship. There's a Ouija board and a crystal ball on the table when you walk in. So of course people are going to be on edge when they enter that space. They're nervous, they're waiting for something to happen, they're thinking of all the bad scenarios that could occur—and those expectations leave a mark. That energy is building into a thought form that mimics the actions people are expecting to see in the room.

The *Queen Mary*'s aggregor was a relatively mild one. As far as I know, it hasn't done anything except just show up in the room occasionally. On an episode in Season 3 of *Kindred Spirits*, though, we found one that was much stronger, and much more dangerous.

Adam and I had been to the Inn at Belvoir Winery in Liberty, Missouri, many times before we filmed a *Kindred Spirits* episode there. The 170-acre property was formerly the location of an Odd Fellows' Home, and it's a known paranormal hotspot. I've hosted many Strange Escapes events there. The owners experienced a significant spike in activity, which seemed like it had a distinctly more negative tone to it, so they asked us to come back and see what was happening there.

The property consists of four main buildings: the orphanage, which has been renovated into the winery and inn, as well as a hospital, a nursing home, and an old folks' home, which are in severe disrepair. Aspiring ghost hunters go there to investigate, but people also go there looking for signs of family members. Over the course of the facility's history, it's estimated that twenty thousand people died there. The owners, Jesse and Melissa, reported feeling a new dark presence, especially in the old folks' home and in the morgue underneath the nursing home. Where there used to be just voices and footsteps, there had now developed a lot of physical contact, like shoving and the pulling of women's hair, as well as things thrown in other rooms.

It didn't take long for us to find strange occurrences at Belvoir. Before we even started our investigation, I put fresh batteries in my recorder, and as soon as I turned it on, the recorder immediately died. "Do you not want us to record you?" Adam asked. Then I saw something at the end of the hallway. It seemed like there was a shadow figure. I had goose bumps. Every hair on my body was standing up at that moment.

So, of course, I walked straight toward it. "Do you ever think about how crazy we are?" I asked Adam. "There's a big shadow man down there. Let me walk over there and put my recorder down next to him."

We made our way through the old folks' home, and into the attached nursing home. But as soon as we got over there, I heard a child's voice in the distance. Adam and I both got the impression that a spirit was trying to help us by leading us out of an area where bad things were happening. What the hell was in there that they were trying to keep us away from?

"I get that you're trying to help us," Adam said, "but we kind of have no choice."

In the nursing home, I saw something dark crawling across the ceiling. I immediately knew it wasn't human. A person doesn't move like that. We both got the impression that whatever it was, it was *definitely* trying to scare us.

And that was all on the first night.

The next day, Chip Coffey and John Tenney joined us to help investigate. We could have gone through the home's records for weeks on end, but John quickly picked up one thing that seemed strange: There had been a man in the home who had exhibited violent behavior—he'd pulled a knife on a nurse before taking his own life. Strangely, we couldn't get a clear idea of his name. Between his hospital records, newspaper clippings of the incident, and his gravestone, this man's name was written six different ways.

That night, we investigated the old folks' home again. There, we picked up an EVP of room 19, but we had trouble finding the room because the numbers were missing on the doors. As we were walking past a room with a nine on the door, I felt something touch my back, not in a scary way, but as though it were telling me to stop there. We started an EVP session.

"We're looking for a man who took his own life," I asked. "Frederick or Fred?"

Fred, we heard.

"We have a number of last names," I said. John listed them.

Lietze.

Fred Lietze died decades ago, and until that moment, his real name had died with him. That was such an incredible moment for me, when we gave that man his name back. It definitely didn't feel like he was the menacing presence.

So we went back into the nursing home.

"It's messing with me already," Chip said, as soon as we walked in. "You wanted us in here, and here we are." He instantly picked up on something dark. And just then, we all heard that child's voice, the same one Adam and I heard the night before, trying to lead us out of there.

"There's something here simply for the fact that there are innocent souls still hanging out here," Chip said, referring to a dark attachment that came into the space because of all the paranormal activity from the ghosts lingering there, and all the people looking for them. "He's coming after the kids."

The darkest activity, and the most violent physical attacks, had happened in the morgue. We went downstairs.

As soon as we entered the morgue, John ducked his head, like he was going to bump into something hanging from the ceiling, only there was nothing there. Adam pulled out the SLS camera. The thing that had been crawling on the ceiling the night before was directly overhead. ("I told Amy that as long as it wasn't crawling across the ceiling I would be fine," John said later. "And the next thing that happened is that we saw something crawling across the ceiling.")

"You have us in the dark," I said in an EVP session. "What is it you want to say to us? What is your name?"

Nothing.

"Do you have a name?" Adam asked.

Nothing.

"Do you know who Chip is?"

I am Chip.

"You could save us the trouble by going right now, on your own," Adam said.

Something grabbed Chip's arm. The response in the recorder was loud and angry, but not words. It got really agitated when we told it to leave. It was trying to collect information about us, and find out what we were capable of. When we realized that it was mimicking what we were doing, to try to get others to interact with it, we realized that we were dealing with an aggregor.

"It's rare," John explained. "It can be born out of the concerns and fears that people have on this compound. It can grow more powerful as it absorbs the massive spiritual energies which cover this place."

After the case was over, John added that the being was responding to our emotions. The more scared we got, the darker and more physical the aggregor's responses became. "It was listening to us and trying to be what we wanted it to be," he said. "Our intent was affecting what was in the building." By intent, he doesn't mean that we *wanted* there to be something terrible there, but rather that we believed something terrible was *already* there, and the more sure we became that this was true, the worse its behavior got. It would only grow stronger as people shared their stories about experiences there. The next people who walk in would likely encounter something even more serious, because their expectations to find something scary will have built upon other peoples' already heightened fears.

It was one of the most negative hauntings I had ever experienced, created by people going in that space over and over, experiencing negative things, and adding to the growing undesirable energy in that place. But as it became stronger, it was able to absorb the energy of other spirits, like the children in the orphanage. That's what Chip meant when he said it was going for the kids.

Our only shot at making this thought form leave was to attack it with its opposite: positive energy. The next day, we gathered everyone we could who had a happy experience with Belvoir. We brought them all together, and asked them to help infuse the nursing home with all of the happy experiences they've had there. "I want you guys to think about the most positive, happy experience with this building," I said, "and I want you to envision that light in you. Inject this building with that positive moment."

"Repeat after me: You are not welcome. You are banished," Adam said. Everyone repeated it.

As we built up our positive intention and infused it into the building, I could feel it working. The space felt lighter. But it will be up to the people there to keep the positive energy flowing, and keep that aggregor away.

SOMETIMES IT'S A GHOST ANIMAL

On one episode of *Ghost Hunters*, we were in Jefferson City, Missouri, at the Missouri State Penitentiary. The penitentiary was opened in 1836, and housed inmates for 168 years before closing in 2004. *Time* once called it "the bloodiest 47 acres in America" for its long history of violent riots and death penalty executions.

Adam and I were investigating together, and we heard a noise from another room. The cameras weren't rolling, though—but given that we can't ask ghosts to only show up when we're filming, we went to investigate anyway.

That the prison has underground "dungeon cells" should give you an idea of what a nasty place it was. So, of course, we headed down a dark hallway to check out that noise.

It got louder and louder as we approached, totally alone. There was no cameraman with us, and no one to know if something really awful happened.

We got closer.

And closer.

And just then, a huge racoon jumped out from inside a trash can, and lunged straight at us.

We have never run so fast in our lives. We basically jumped down an entire flight of stairs. It was insane.

So yeah, it's not always a ghost. But it is definitely always scary.

Chapter 7

THERE'S NO RIGHT WAY TO FIND SPIRITS

IF YOU'VE EVER done an investigation, you already know that there's no "right way" or "wrong way" to look for evidence of the paranormal. There are ways that sometimes produce more reliable results than others, but those methods vary from person to person. Maybe you have a knack for asking the right questions and get really strong EVP responses—or maybe you're excellent at noticing minuscule anomalies on video that other people don't usually see. I have methods I tend to go back to more than others, but the researcher in me loves to learn about new techniques and evolve my investigative strategies over time. It's so exciting bringing in other researchers and paranormal experts because of their different investigative viewpoints. When we put our heads together, we often come up with unusual strategies that Adam and I could not fully execute on our own. On a case during Season 3 of *Kindred Spirits*, a deck of tarot cards turned out to be the key in finding out who was causing the activity in a home.

Sharon called us to her home in Willington, Connecticut, because she feared for the lives of her two living children. She had survived unimaginable losses: One of her children had died in childbirth, and two others died in car crashes as adults. Sharon thought she had some kind of dark attachment to her that was causing so much tragedy in her family. "Bad things happen to everybody, but not like me," she said. "Who has to bury three of their children?"

She saw orbs in the home, which she thought might be tied to her daughter Miranda, who had died a few years earlier. Her son Brady heard voices trying to talk to him in his bedroom, and her daughter Anna heard tapping noises in her room and a disembodied voice once asked her for help.

Anna had a deck of tarot cards in her bedroom that had once belonged to Miranda. She had given them to Anna on her eighteenth birthday. That was the last time she saw Miranda alive. Anna tried to use them, she said, "but when I would try to communicate with them I would scare myself." In that same conversation, Anna told us that her sister and her mother had had a difficult relationship, and weren't speaking when Miranda was killed.

Because we suspected Miranda might be in the home, Adam and I decided to use those tarot cards during that night's investigation as a trigger object. Sometimes, when we think the activity is coming from a certain person, we'll use their belongings to help draw them out and give the spirits something familiar to latch on to. That night, it worked. As soon as we hooked up the tarot cards to the proximity sensor, which indicates when an entity is making contact with an object, the sensors went off.

"Is this your house?" I asked in an EVP session. "I feel like it's probably very frustrating to be in this position where no one can see you and no one can hear you, but we can try with what we've brought here to see you and hear you."

I'm right here, we heard back.

That voice came through so loudly that it startled us. The person was clearly angry, but we couldn't tell where the anger was coming from. If Miranda was there, it would make sense that she'd be trying to fix the situation with her family now. But we couldn't determine if it really was her, or what she might want. The rest of the investigation that night was quiet.

So, we brought in Dana Newkirk to help us. Dana, who is a paranormal investigator and also a practicing witch, uses her tarot deck in all her investigations. "When we investigate, my tools of choice are always the meta-physical ones," she said. "I'll pull cards and just say, *What is going on here?*" The cards she draws from the deck help give Dana insight into what's happening, especially with the energy in a space.

That night, she pulled the Temperance card first. "It's the card of balance," Dana said. "Something has become unbalanced in this house." Next, the Ace of Cups, an indicator of emotional unbalance. "The Ace is saying specifically in this house all emotions are in a state of flux because of this imbalance," she explained. "The emotional unbalance is causing the activity in the house."

We started another EVP session. "Can you tell us your name?" I asked.

Randa. Anna explained that was Miranda's nickname.

"Do you think this house can be fixed?"

Yes I do.

We had done work with Sharon upstairs to help push out whatever darkness she felt was attached to her. But the key to helping Miranda's ghost was to get her and her mother to have a conversation. We brought Sharon downstairs into Anna's room, where we had been using the tarot cards the night before. Anna had explained to us earlier that she and her mother had a similarly difficult dynamic like Miranda had with Sharon, and there was a lot of tension between them. We suspected that Miranda was staying in the home to try to help her sister.

"All right Miranda, we know you're down here," I said in an EVP session. "We talked to you. We brought your mom. Is that what you want us to do to fix things here?"

Yes, she answered.

"Do you want your mom and Anna to have a loving relationship?"

I do.

We asked Sharon to give a message to Miranda. "I love her a lot," she said. "I miss her. I'm sorry for what happened to her. I'm fighting for her every day. She's my girl. She's still my girl."

"Miranda, I know you're here to facilitate this," Adam said. "We do appreciate you being here and helping us with this task because it is very important. And when you are ready to go you can go."

At that, we all heard footsteps above us. Heavy steps, walking across the room, like someone was leaving.

"Miranda," he continued, "are you still here?"

Nothing. No response at all. Every time Miranda spoke to us that night, the K-II had lit up. At that moment, it was completely dark and it remained that way.

In that case, using Miranda's tarot deck as a trigger object was the key that unlocked the rest of the case for us. The same happened in Season 4, when we investigated the Randolph County Asylum in Winchester, Indiana. We made contact with Harry "Peg" Dunn—remember that prankster who would sometimes scare people for fun?—

because we used his fake leg as a trigger object. Even in the afterlife, he still had an attachment to the thing that helped him walk in life.

Sometimes, though, the object in question doesn't actually have to be attached to a specific spirit to be helpful in making contact. That's especially true of haunted objects, which have a surprisingly useful role in paranormal investigation. There have been many times when the answer to a case was that an object was haunted— like at the May-Stringer House Museum in Brooksville, Florida, where tour guides reported dark activity that turned out to be tied to a haunted trunk in the museum, which we investigated on Season 4 of *Kindred*. But in other instances, we intentionally bring in high-energy artifacts to act as trigger objects in an investigation.

In addition to producing *Hellier* and being paranormal researchers, Dana and Greg Newkirk also specialize in curating and studying haunted objects. They run the Traveling Museum of the Paranormal & Occult, which is a massive collection of artifacts that are either haunted or have strong ties to the supernatural. (Before you ask, yes, they *do* keep all the haunted stuff in their house.)

"We have a much different view about haunted objects than pretty much anyone we've ever met," Greg said. "When most people think of a haunted object, they think of scary antique toys like Annabelle"—the reportedly haunted doll famously investigated by Ed and Lorraine

Warren, the story of which has been made into three horror movies since 2014—"and these things that want to hurt you and drag you to hell.

"That has not been our experience at all," Greg continued. "I think the reason we haven't had that experience is that we've never set that intention. Our motto has always been 'curiosity through fear.' If you are afraid of something, you're never going to learn anything from it."

Greg and Dana have brought artifacts from their traveling museum to many Strange Escapes events, everywhere from New England to Hawaii, to cruises through the Caribbean. The collection includes items like a dark mirror that shows people their worst fears, and a replica of a wooden carving of a crone that was so volatile and brought so much negative activity with it that the original had to be returned to the woods where it was found, and quieted through a magic ritual that Dana led with a hundred other witches around the world.

Scary stories aside, the Newkirks and their haunted collection have added essential components to some truly fascinating investigations. Once, at a Strange Escapes on Mackinac Island in Michigan, they brought an old wedding dress from the 1800s with them. The dress had been given to them by a man in New England who kept seeing a woman in white walk through his house. He asked Greg and Dana for help, and they responded that he should watch where the woman was walking to try to see what she wanted. That's how he found a chest in his attic that contained a wedding dress. As soon as he gave the dress to the museum, the haunting in his house stopped.

However, Greg and Dana had never really gotten much activity from the dress itself. All of that changed on the island. They used it as part of an Estes Method investigation, and a distinctly female presence in the hotel was drawn to it. She talked about how she was a guest at the hotel who had come with her family. The ghost was focused on the wedding dress because she herself couldn't wait to get married.

Here's where it gets weird, though. The Mackinac spirit woman's excitement about the wedding dress drew the attention of the bride herself. The owner of the dress *finally* started talking, because the local spirit Greg and Dana communicated with brought her to it. The ghostly hotel guest facilitated a conversation between the Newkirks and another ghost they hadn't been able to reach until that point. It was like the dress drew out a ghost at the hotel, and then the ghost at the hotel drew out the owner of the dress.

Haunted objects, Dana explained, act as a way to focus intention in an investigation, not just for the living people there, but for the ghosts, too. "If you've got an object that has had so much psychic impression and so much energy projected into it," she said, it can act as a psychic trigger object. "It creates energy and a space for things to communicate. It's almost as if it draws them out because they're like, *I don't know what that is.* It spikes a lot of curiosity from the spirit side."

We've utilized items like that in many investigations. They can be especially useful in situations where we're revisiting places we've investigated before, like the *Queen Mary*. These haunted objects carry different energy and so they attract different energy than we experienced on previous visits.

Building on prior investigations, and having the freedom to experiment with new techniques, is what I love so much about long-term cases. It's rare to get to study a place over a span of years, but it does happen sometimes. My favorite of all those places is the Mount Washington Hotel, in Bretton Woods, New Hampshire.

Every time I go, I learn more about the spirits residing there. Strange Escapes hosts an event there every fall, but I also go back several other times a year, just on little vacations. It really is like my own Haunted Mansion, except without Walt Disney's face on a statue singing about "grim grinning ghosts" who "come out to socialize." Well, the ghosts are definitely there and they're definitely socializing—but whether Walt himself is there...probably not.

At this point, I've heard dozens upon dozens of ghost stories about the place: from the staff, from other guests, from the weirdos who come to our ghost events, and from my friends. Without even intentionally doing it, I've been conducting my own multiyear case study of the hotel, just from my own observations and the information I've collected from my visits there.

What I've found is there is something really strange going on in this hotel, especially in the kind of spirits it attracts.

The first time I ever went to the Mount Washington, it was for an event I was helping to run, before I'd started Strange Escapes. I was walking around the hotel with Britt Griffith, with whom I was running the event. It was the middle of the night, but we wanted to get an idea of the space. The last room we walked through was the ballroom, and as we were departing I said, "Well, hopefully this place is haunted." Just then, we both heard this loud laughter. It was definitely coming from a woman in the ballroom with us. The only problem? It was something like 3 a.m. and we were completely alone. It was within the first hour of me being there. I still get chills thinking about it. I didn't realize it at the time, but that was the beginning of what would be almost like a friendship with the hotel. I feel like I've forged a connection with that place, just from how many times I've been there, and all of the experiences I've had there since.

Princess Carolyn, the wife of Joseph Stickney (the man who built the hotel and whose portrait is and isn't hanging in the lobby), is definitely not the only ghost in the Mount

Washington. Her spirit is always there, in that there's always a table set for her in the dining room and there are portraits of her hanging on the walls. These portraits include one of her standing on the secret balcony where she would watch all the women go into the dining room and appraise their clothing so that she could put on something even nicer and be the best dressed at dinner. But her *spirit* isn't always there—or, at least, she doesn't make herself available to chat all the time.

In addition to the times I've spoken to the princess, I've also spoken to a grumpy man in the Princess Room, who really didn't want anything to do with speaking to us. I've had lights go on and off in my room, over and over, because the light switch kept flipping up after I moved it down. I've had loud, scary knocks on the door in the middle of the night, even though there was no one anywhere to be found in the hallway.

Once, Adam was leading an investigation in one of the old turret suites that we are no longer allowed into. They are in such disrepair that it's not safe to be in there. He was telling the group about safety precautions, and while he spoke, he noticed a woman staring at him. She had black hair, was wearing a red sweatshirt and gray sweatpants, and was holding a Diet Coke bottle. He said, "Can I help you? You can go and investigate."

"No," she said. "I want to stay with you."

"Okay," Adam responded. "You heard the rules, right?"

"No," she replied.

He told her where it was safe to go. "And don't go in this room," he said, trying to make light of the awkward exchange, "because you could trip and fall through the skylight, and die."

She looked at him. "That'd be okay," she said.

At that point, Adam noticed that the soda bottle she was holding was filthy. "Hold on a second," he said, and turned his head to check on some people investigating in another room. As he did, he realized the woman hadn't been wearing the lanyard we gave to all attendees, and that she must have been crashing the event. "Hey, can I see…" he said, as he turned his head back to her.

She was gone. And there was no way she would have had time to make it out the door to the suite, and no way she could have done it silently, even if she had snuck out. The door, and the floor, were far too noisy.

Maybe she was who they were searching for all along.

Hearing about that experience still gives me goose bumps, but the creepiest encounter I've heard about the Mount Washington Hotel happened to other friends of mine.

Kiel and Sarah Patrick, who founded the Kiel James Patrick clothing company, have been visiting the Mount Washington for years. In fact, they've rented the Princess Room to celebrate New Year's Eve several different times. On New Year's Eve 2016, they went to the bash in the ballroom, and then had friends back up to that room for an afterparty. (I should note: They didn't choose the room for the ghosts. At that time, spirits weren't on their radar at all. The room has a big, open living space that's really nice for entertaining small groups.)

That night, an older man named Steve found his way into their group. He kept talking about how high he was, and saying he wanted to talk to the girls. He wasn't welcome, but he refused to leave, and was eventually escorted out by one of their friends.

Steve snuck back in for a second time when someone opened the door to leave, and Kiel eventually called security to have him removed. He left on his own, and security couldn't find any traces of him afterward.

Weird, but okay.

Almost three years later, Kiel and Sarah came back up to New Hampshire for Strange Escapes. While the investigations were happening, they were already in bed. Suddenly, their night-light went out, and the bathroom door slammed. At the same time, I was texting them asking if they were up. All of the EVPs coming through in the Princess Room were from a guy named Steve, asking for Kiel, saying that he was so high and he wanted to talk to the girls.

The group didn't know Kiel and Sarah. There was no chance anyone in the Princess Room had heard their story from years before.

The man who was at their party had been a ghost.

Aside from being supremely creepy, their experience raises another interesting thing I've observed about the hotel: The ghosts remember you. When I go back, I feel like they always know who I am, and that we're picking up where we left off. Many times, I've captured EVPs that say *Hi Amy*, in the Princess Room and other spaces. Other people have reported similar experiences. One of our "Escapees," as I like to call them, swears there's a presence in the lobby bathrooms that remembers her from visit to visit. And Greg Newkirk, when he was doing a repetition EVP experiment where he kept saying "knock, knock," trying to get someone to answer *Who's there?*, once got a ghost who was so tired of the gag that he said, in the clearest response of the night, *Oh, not this joke again.*

John Tenney has hypothesized that in addition to these spirits who seem to recognize us when we return, there may be ghosts who use the building for recreation, just like we do. "Because the place is a resort, the ghosts are using it as a resort, too," he said. That's why so many of the spirits we encounter are transient, and we don't encounter them again, because a hotel is by nature a transient space. "If you come at certain times, you're going to get a person because they're going there like they would in their lifetime," he explained. "They're sticking to their holiday timeline. They did something over and over in life, and they didn't stop once they died. They keep going back to visit."

He tends to see the most activity at the hotel late at night, when someone ahead of him in a hallway will turn a corner and vanish. "If you have the ability to go anywhere because you're not locked into a physical form anymore, why wouldn't you want to go to the places you loved when you were alive?" John said. I think that's why Princess Carolyn doesn't often want to talk to people who are trying to make contact with her. Think about it: If you had people disturbing your vacation every five minutes to ask the same three questions, you'd get tired of it, too.

Dana Newkirk thinks that the living people who visit the hotel have something to do with the kind of ghosts who visit, too. "I think it's very possible that people are coming here knowing it's haunted, and wanting to communicate with what's here. They're bringing that intention right into the space, and helping change the frequency of it," she said. "You can't roll up here and *not* wonder if the hotel is haunted. Even if you've never heard that, you can't pull up to this hotel and not think it."

She's not wrong. The gleaming white hotel, with its vivid red roof, makes a dramatic first impression. It's set back from the road, with this long, winding driveway up to the front, and sits in stark contrast to Mount Washington behind it, which is the tallest peak on the East Coast and is almost always capped with snow, even in the summer. There is something simultaneously alluring and arresting about the place. Even with its imposing stature, the building draws you in. I wonder if anyone has ever driven past the hotel and been able to resist wondering what it was like inside.

Another thing that's curious to me is that the most vivid paranormal experiences tend to happen with spirits from a narrow time period. There are so many stories, like Adam's and Kiel and Sarah's, that feature people specifically from the 1970s and 1980s (at least it seems that's when they're from, judging from their clothing and demeanor). I almost think there's some kind of weird time-travel dimensional shift going on in the hotel that connects the present to that era. That's the part of the experience that almost does feel like *The Shining*, that there's another time period happening simultaneously with our reality in the same space. What is it specifically about that time period? Did something happen there that we don't know about? Eventually I hope to learn the answer, but I don't know it now.

It might seem odd that the spirits I've observed are largely *not* from the Mount Washington's heyday as a grand hotel in the early twentieth century. But that's the thing about locations that have strong ties to time periods or historical events. When some investigators go in, they tend to focus only on that era. In those cases, their pre-conceived notions of what time period the activity might be tied to often exclude decades (or even sometimes centuries) of history attached to the location outside of one big landmark event.

When Adam and I investigated the Farnsworth House in Gettysburg, Pennsylvania, in Season 3 of *Kindred*, even though we were investigating a place that had major historical significance in the Civil War, the resolution of the case had nothing to do with the war at all. (Spoiler alert: It was a haunted mirror.)

At Mount Washington, John thinks the ties to a specific kind of ghost could have something to do with the fact that people enjoy themselves so much in the space that the spirits derive pleasure from that, too. The hotel is generally a happy gathering place, hosting weddings and gala events hundreds of times a year. The ghosts could be responding to our heightened energy. We don't know, he said, but our "extreme emotional state of being happy might very much be like being drunk to them.

"Like all of a sudden, they have the power to manifest, and someone's talking to them, and everybody's having a good time, and all of a sudden they don't know why they're communicating," John continued. "When you talk to a drunken person, they only give you half answers and they meander down roads they don't really mean to meander down. It seems a lot of the time when you're at a party and you're communicating with a spirit, especially at the Mount Washington, they're almost communicating in the same fashion."

Mount Washington has a lot of secrets in its walls, and I'm still discovering them. There's a bar in the basement that was an honest-to-goodness speakeasy during Prohibition. There's a trapdoor in the floor of that bar that leads to a room underneath. I've been in there, but it's no longer accessible. The same with the turret rooms that weren't renovated. That hotel has a lot of hiding places, and the ghosts act accordingly. I'm strangely attracted to it. It's a happy place to me. Once, Charlotte and I were there with guests in just two other rooms in the hotel. We had the whole place to ourselves. You might think it would be spooky, but I felt totally at ease. But then again, I like weird stuff…and I think there's more to the story that we haven't learned yet.

"Not only is it a hotel for humans, but it seems to be a hotel for ghosts," John said. "They're checking in, staying for a while, and checking back out." He thinks the very nature of the building adds to the supernatural experiences there. "People go to hotels a lot of times when they have secrets—to have affairs, to get away from a person they don't like, to sneak off for a romantic weekend. The ghosts are doing the same things, and they're carrying secrets along with them." That's part of why the encounters with ghosts in the hotel are almost always very brief. "Sometimes they'll start talking to you, and realize they're giving up a secret, and stop talking. But now you've got the inklings of that secret, and you might never get a chance to resolve it, because now that ghost might never come back."

There's another case I've been working on just as long as I've been learning about the Mount Washington Hotel. That one is a little bit closer to my home. It involves one particular ghost I've been searching for for over a decade.

The Lizzie Borden House, in Fall River, Massachusetts, is the site of one of the country's most infamous crimes. Even if you don't know much about New England history, you've probably heard the rhyme about the ax and the forty whacks. Andrew and Abby Borden were murdered with an ax in 1892, and Andrew's daughter (Abby's step-daughter) Lizzie was tried and acquitted of the crime. The trial became one of the most widely circulated news stories of the day, and even though Lizzie was set free, she was never truly forgiven by the public as they suspected she was the true killer.

Because I live in the area, I go to investigate that house often. Over the last ten or so years, I've been there to investigate probably a dozen times, both with small groups and to film TV episodes. In Season 3 of *Kindred*, we investigated the Lizzie Borden House because one of the guides, Sue, felt as though she was being specifically targeted with a different kind of activity. We made contact with who we believe is Andrew Borden, but we found that the activity we were investigating was really coming from Sue's grandparents, who were trying to send her a message that they were waiting for her ailing father when he was ready to move on. He passed away just days after we investigated the home. I hope knowing his parents were waiting for him made Sue's pain a little bit more bearable.

Over the years, I've witnessed a lot of paranormal activity in the home where the murders took place. It's a great spot to bring people who are just learning to investigate, because something almost always happens there. The more I investigate the Borden House, the more I realize that even though there is strong activity, none of the activity is interacting with me. My guess is that what's occurring in the house is a highly residual haunt, where there is a lot of energy in the space, but that it's not necessarily from active ghosts. I think the supernatural energy is increased by people coming into the house knowing about the murders and the legends about Lizzie, and they bring all their own speculations and hopes to see something spooky. There are artifacts and newspaper clippings all over the home and the gift shop. The energy of the Borden House is fed often, and fed well, by one of the most notorious true crime cases in American history.

In all the times I've been to that home, I've never spoken to Lizzie Borden. But on Season 4 of *Kindred*, Adam and I were finally able to investigate another place that cracked the mystery wide open for us.

Maplecroft, in another part of Fall River, is the home that Lizzie and her sister Emma moved to after the death of her parents. They had inherited the family's money, and bought a much larger home that served as a sanctuary away from the prying eyes of the town.

Lizzie lived in that home for more than thirty years, until her death in 1927. When we arrived to film an episode there, Maplecroft had never been investigated by ghost hunters. We were the first people to investigate the space in over ninety years.

The woman who owns the Lizzie Borden House purchased Maplecroft, and was preparing to open the building to the public. The previous owners had told her it wasn't haunted, but once she and her employees spent time there, they started witnessing a *lot* of activity. They would hear loud footsteps, the disembodied voice of a woman, and laughter at strange times.

Before we started investigating, we brought Chip Coffey in to get his impressions of the home. So he wouldn't see where he was or get any clues that might influence his reading, we brought him in blindfolded.

"All of a sudden I'm very agitated and upset," he said. "There's a sense of being out of control. I'm being hit by every kind of emotion. I'm trying to get a grip on my emotions and I just can't. I hear: *Stop, leave me alone.*"

He was picking up the spirit of a woman who was getting increasingly angry. "*'You all think you know everything,'*" he reported her saying. "*'You know nothing about me.'*"

"She's screaming, *'DON'T HELP ME,'*" Chip added, then repeated more of her words. "*'You got him blindfolded. You think you're smart. I don't care what you think. I have to look right. I won't crack. I'm sorry.'*"

As part of our research, we spoke with historian Christopher Daley about Lizzie. "It's America's Jack the Ripper case," he said, "and people are going to be talking about it forever."

Christopher went on to explain why Lizzie chose to remain in Fall River, when almost the entire town had turned on her, suspecting her of murdering her parents even though she had been acquitted of the crime. "She said, 'When the truth comes out about this murder, I want to be living in Fall River so I can walk downtown and meet those of my friends who have been cutting me down all these years.'"

He also told us a key piece of information. After the trial, Lizzie adopted a new name, Lizbeth. That's what's on her gravestone, even though her birth name is Lizzie, and it's how she chose to be addressed for all her adult life.

The night before, we had gotten an EVP response of the name Lizzie Borden. We really thought we might have been talking to her—but besides that one answer, she hadn't said much of anything. From what Chip indicated, she did not care to speak more.

Thinking she had given us her name as a sassy response, Adam suggested approaching that night's investigation in a different way, by removing all the things in the home that discussed murder in any way. "We need to make her comfortable if we're going to get any answers," he said. "We need to make this feel like her home."

So that evening, we set about making Maplecroft an ax murder–free zone, narrating our actions as we went so she would see and hear what we were doing. We made sure to speak to her using the name she chose to go by, as a sign of respect, and we reassured her that we only had good intentions and didn't want to exploit or sensationalize her past. Then, we set up a spirit box experiment designed to make Lizbeth feel as comfortable as possible. I went upstairs to a sitting room, while Adam stayed downstairs and asked questions through a walkie-talkie.

"My friend Amy is upstairs," he said. "I'd love for you to reach out to her please. Can you tell her your name?"

Lizbeth.

"You're going to have a lot of people coming in here to try to talk to you. And most of those people are going to try to talk about—"

Directly.

"Yes, they're going to talk to you directly."

I'm lost.

"The people that own this house now also own the house—"

Don't say anything. It's not me.

"People are going to ask you about what happened on Second Street. We're trying to warn you and let you know, to see if that's okay with you."

Please talk to them. Are you there?

"So you're saying it's okay for people to come talk to you about your past?"

Come back.

"What would you like to talk about?"

I felt someone walking through the room, but no one was there.

"Do you miss someone, Lizbeth, from your past?"

You get used to it. I'm upset.

"What are you upset about?"

Stop. Stop it. Alone. I tried.

We had just had a full conversation with the ghost of Lizbeth Borden, maybe for the first time ever. I was hearing full sentences, which almost never happens with ghost replies in EVP sessions or spirit box experiments. It was hard to hear, though: She seemed so conflicted and lonely.

I think the only reason that Lizbeth chose to speak to us is that we broke the ice with her, and treated her with kindness, even though we were looking for one of the most sought-after spirits of all time, who may or may not be a murderer. We don't know for sure. I do know that she has a lot of people calling out for her, and I haven't heard of another time when she answered.

By the end of it, I felt like Lizbeth was my friend. So even though one of the producers was really pushing for us to ask her if she was guilty, we wouldn't do it. We would have violated the trust we'd built with her, and everything we had worked for. Adam and I never asked her if she did it. If we did, we would have been lying to her the whole time when we promised not to talk about the murders.

The Lizzie Borden case may be one of the most notorious American true crime stories, but we'll never have any answers—and that's because Lizbeth wanted it that way. There's a law firm in Boston that has all of her files and the paperwork on the case, and they are locked up to this day. She made that firm sign paperwork stating they would guard that information in perpetuity, and never unseal those files. So the answer is sitting just over fifty miles from where the crime happened, and it will never be revealed.

THE LEGEND OF THE GHOST BREAD

To me, one of the best parts of filming cases in New England is that I don't have to be away from my daughter. While we were filming at Maplecroft, because it was close by, Charlotte would come to the house after school was done for the day.

(I've been bringing Charlotte to haunted places since before she was born. One day, she'll write her own book about growing up with ghosts. I can't wait to read about all of this from her perspective.)

On that day, we were doing some really intensive work that needed my full attention, and Charlotte wanted to be entertained. "Charlotte, here, look at this," our production manager, Sean Nichols, said. He was holding a plastic baguette that was in a display of fake food on the mantel. "This is ghost bread."

"Ghost bread?" she asked, lighting up.

"Yeah," he said. "You take it and hide it somewhere, and ghosts will come eat it. They love it."

Charlotte grabbed the loaf and ran upstairs. "Gho-ooosts," we heard her calling, "I have ghoooost breeeeead."

After she hid it, we heard her coming back down the stairs. As she did, Sean ran up the back stairway, grabbed the bread, and snuck back down without her noticing.

"Mom," Charlotte said. "Let's go see if the ghosts ate the ghost bread."

When we got back up there, it had disappeared. She couldn't believe what had just happened.

To this day, we take that ghost bread on every case we investigate, and we make sure it's placed somewhere in a shot that makes it to air. So next time you're watching us hunt for ghosts, make sure to hunt for ghost bread, too.

Chapter 8
BEWARE OF HITCHHIKING GHOSTS
(Or Don't)

SO HERE'S THE thing. I collect creepy dolls.

In fact, I'm kind of obsessed with them.

It's weird. I know. People always ask me why I buy them, when there's a danger that the dolls are haunted or have negative energy attached to them. But those same people refuse to buy any antiques at all because they're so afraid of what residual energy might come with them. And that, I think, is even weirder.

In all honesty, I just feel sorry for those dolls. I see them and I feel sad that people are looking at them like they're ugly and scary, so I adopt them and give them a loving place to live. Well, at least *I* love them. Charlotte is absolutely creeped out by them.

Recently, I picked one up in an antiques store. It was a 1920s bed doll—a specific type of large doll made for adults, to sit on beds and decorate them, usually made with human hair on their heads. I didn't know anything about the doll other than that it was old and weird, so it was for me. I brought it up to the counter and the cashier said, "Oh, that's the doll we keep finding on the floor every morning."

So yeah, of course it was haunted. I can't help it. I just gravitate toward these things.

The doll hasn't displayed any activity at my house. I think she just wanted a good home. But like I said, people still worry a lot about me bringing residual energy into my house. One of the most common questions people ask me is how I protect myself from bringing anything home, or from having spirits attach themselves to me. The answer is: I don't. Or, more accurately, I just don't worry about it very much.

People who haven't spent as much time around ghosts as I have tend to focus on the danger and fear they associate with the paranormal. That totally makes sense. So much of the representation of the supernatural in pop culture is created to scare you, and make you feel like you could be exposed to something that will attach itself to you and cause terrible things to happen.

Scary movies are one thing. You can avoid them if you want to. But those ideas are everywhere, even at

Walt Disney World. "There's a little matter I forgot to mention," the Ghost Host narrator says at the end of the Haunted Mansion ride. "Beware of hitchhiking ghosts!"

In the storyline of the ride, there are "999 happy haunts" in the mansion, but there's room for one more— and at the end, you find out that the ghosts have chosen you as lucky one thousand. "They'll haunt you until you return," he says. "Now I will raise the safety bar, and a ghost will follow you home!"

As you've seen on *Kindred Spirits* and other paranormal investigation shows, haunted houses in real life aren't the same as the ones you see on TV. There's a lot fewer red glowing eyes and a lot more sitting in the dark waiting for a noise from the other room. In the vast majority of cases, not only can real life ghosts not hurt you, they aren't even trying to.

So, when a ghost *has* followed me home—you knew that was coming, right?—I haven't been that concerned about it.

I was in Charleston, South Carolina, for an episode of *Ghost Hunters*. Jason Hawes and I were investigating the Old City Jail together. We were in this strange room that wasn't quite a cell, when at the same time, Jay got a scratch on his neck and I felt something warm around my legs, almost like someone was hugging them. That was really the only activity we got.

After we were done with the investigation, I was doing a recap of my impressions of the night. A producer was asking me questions and recording my responses. It turns out I had been in one of the rooms where wives and children, if they had nowhere else to go, would have to live while their husbands and fathers were incarcerated. The conditions in a place like that, in 1802 when that jail was built, would have been intolerable. Pregnant women gave birth there, with no one to help them. Kids starved to death in those rooms.

I didn't know where we had been. So when the producer asked me how I felt, having been in a room where so many innocent people suffered, I lost it. I was sixteen weeks pregnant with Charlotte and very emotional, and I could *not* take the idea of being in that kind of space without knowing it. I started crying. "Stop filming," I said. "I don't even want to talk about this. This is awful." All of a sudden, the producer got scratched—and she continued to get scratched for the rest of the time we were in the jail. It was almost like whoever was there was angry that she had upset me, and was being protective.

When I got home, everything seemed fine—until I was upstairs in my bathroom, and I saw this little shadow run down the hallway from my bedroom to what was going to be Charlotte's room. My house was definitely not haunted, so it got my attention right away. But I didn't see it again, and I flew back to Charleston to finish up the episode.

While I was gone, a friend was in my house, helping me out with a few things. She sent me a text: "Amy, I just saw a little shadow run down your upstairs hallway." And later, she saw something fly across my bedroom. I hadn't talked to her at all, and she was reporting the exact same thing I had experienced—so I knew something weird was happening. A spirit had followed me home from that jail.

When I put that little shadow together with whatever had hugged me around my legs, as a kid would, it seemed like it was a child trying to get attention. When I got home, I had a talk with that little boy or girl. "You can stay as long as you want," I said, "as long as you're not scaring anyone or disrupting anything. I'm about to be a mom myself." I saw the shadow a few more times, but eventually, it was gone.

See? You can have a ghost in your house and have it totally not be scary.

Investigators all have their own ways of mentally or physically preparing to work on a case. Before they go into a haunted place, a lot of people pray, or do some intention-based energy work to feel as though they're layering on protections. Some people use crystals or some kind of amulet as a token of protection. It's all about what you need to do to feel ready to enter the space.

Personally, I don't do any of those things. The way I protect myself is by knowing that I am too strong to let that happen. When I go into a space, I go in knowing that I am enough. If I'm relying on some kind of religious medal, or prayer, or crystal, it leaves me open to vulnerability. If I lose that item, or forget to say what I usually say, I will feel weaker. I don't ever want to put myself in that position.

The other factor is that I know that if something like that does happen, and a ghost follows me home, I am fully capable of handling the situation. A ghost is not going to permanently attach itself to me and cause negative things to happen in my life, which is a fear people often express on cases we're investigating (like Sharon feared was happening at her home in Connecticut from the previous chapter) and in my personal life (like how people criticize me for buying antiques).

Don't forget: Ghosts have free will, just like we do. If one of them chooses to come home with me, I can't exactly stop that. Some of these spirits have an intense need to get a message out there. If you're the first hope they've had in a long time, they might just follow you.

"If they're intelligent and they can go where they want," Adam said, "what's to say they can't come with you?"

Maybe that person isn't done talking, or maybe you're the first person to listen to that spirit in decades. You might decide the conversation is over, but that ghost might be like, *Wait a minute, I wasn't done.* There's a chance they might want to continue that exchange. That's what I always tell aspiring investigators they need to be prepared for. If you're going into a haunted place, you can't necessarily dictate what you're going to find, or how those spirits are going to act.

To address that, you just have to set a boundary. As Adam and I were leaving an investigation at Trans-Allegheny Lunatic Asylum in Weston, West Virginia, we both had a very strong sense that something was with us. We stopped and looked at each other. I asked, "Are you feeling that?" And he said, "Yeah, there's something behind us." So we both turned around, and said firmly, "You have to stay here. You cannot come with us." Whatever it was listened to us, and stayed behind.

That said, my attitude when I walk into a haunted place has everything to do with the outcome.

I strongly believe that your intention controls your experience in a place. It all boils down to your perspective, your vibe, and your energy. I walk in with the mindset that I have a job to do, and when I leave, I don't take my work home with me. Someone who walks in afraid, insecure in their own abilities, might attract a different kind of interaction.

But though you can control your intention, you can't control the people around you, whether they're alive or dead. Just like living people, there are times when ghosts act inappropriately in any number of ways. Whatever was attached to that haunted trunk in the May-Stringer House in Florida was kind of a jerk. He would pull the tour guide's hair, and touch her constantly, though he knew she was afraid and it bothered her. It pinched me and Adam several times, in sharp, deliberate grabs. One of the ways a ghost could have a differing opinion on appropriate behavior is thinking it's okay to follow you home. I think people automatically assume that's an attachment when it happens. In reality, though, I have seen very few actual spirit attachments to people.

Attachments, more often than not, will happen with objects. That trunk in Florida definitely had an attachment, and that's why the activity was strongly concentrated around it. But a spirit can have an affinity for an item and be inspired to communicate when they see it, but not be tied to it. "I believe there's a scale of attachment when it comes to an object," Adam said. "You moved that trunk, it went with the trunk. But then you have objects that are just recognizable, like jewelry or a love letter, something that's sentimental—ghosts can react to those objects but not be physically bound to them."

People tend to hold on to items like their family rosary beads, he believes, because of the energy and intention their owners infused in them. "They are constantly putting energy into that piece of jewelry: wishing for things, praying for things, focusing on things. They hold a lot of energy, and when they are passed down to generations, that's why people keep them."

"My granny's Bible," Adam said. "I know she spent time and energy reading it, writing in it, and holding it. If you could go and pick that Bible up and sit long enough, I believe that you could feel it. They're there with you."

Greg and Dana Newkirk believe that a lot of the haunted objects in their collection have become haunted because of some kind of negative experience associated with the owner. "There's an element with most of the stuff that's given to us where I think people have manifested some sort of fear or trauma in them, and psychically or psychologically stored it in this item," Greg said. "There's something about this item that they've used it as a carrier for their trauma." That's why, he believes, the majority of their collection doesn't display any kind of disruptive negative energy and coexists peacefully in their house. "Ninety-five percent of stuff people give us doesn't ever do anything strange for us."

"On one level, it's a psychological coping mechanism," Dana said. "But there's also something going on on a paranormal level, where whatever the process of releasing that psychically imbues it into an object."

They hold on to those inert items because they were likely meaningful to someone in a significant way. "We have shelves full of stuff that has never so much as fallen down funny," Greg said. "But the other 5 percent can be very, very interesting."

THE MYSTERY OF THE BURNING DOLL

I bought my first-ever creepy doll when I was twelve or thirteen years old, living in Petaluma, California. There was an antiques store just up the street from us, and I would go in there and shop all the time.

I fell in love with a bed doll in the store that was so expensive, way beyond any amount of money I had as an adolescent. I think it was like a hundred dollars. The shop owner let me put it on layaway, and I would go every week and give her my allowance money.

When I had finally paid it off, I brought the doll home, and put it on a shelf in my bedroom.

And that's when it started trying to burn down my house.

One day, I came home to smell burning in my room. *That's weird*, I thought, and looked around for the source. On the shelf above the doll, there was a scorch mark.

A few days later, I smelled burning in my room again. This time, when I picked it up, I saw smoke coming from the doll. Her dress was smoldering, almost like paper slowly burning.

So of course, I put it in my closet and called my Auntie Roxi.

She decided that we should have a séance over the doll to try to figure out what was going on. We did a ritual—I can't really remember what we did—and she tried to tune in to the doll psychically. According to her psychic reading, the woman who previously owned the doll had been very sick, basically dying. There had been a fire burning in the fireplace in her house, and the last thing this woman saw when she was passing away, according to my aunt, was that an ember had gotten very close to the doll, and she was worried about the doll catching on fire. Somehow, the doll had been infused with some kind of fire association as her owner died.

I have no way to verify any of it. But that experience definitely triggered my interest in haunted objects. I ended up collecting dozens of those dolls. Eventually, I sold them because I ran out of space.

That original doll? Well, my cat took an intense dislike to it, and ruined it in a very specific way that only cats can. Maybe he was trying to put out the fires. I don't know. But that poor doll ended up—of all places—in the trash burn pile.

Chapter 9

A HAUNTED PRISON ISN'T THE SCARIEST PLACE YOU CAN VISIT

A HAUNTED ASYLUM, though—that's another story.

If you close your eyes and think of the absolute scariest place you can imagine, what do you see? Rusted bars covering the entrance to crumbling cells? A dark cemetery, filled with moldering crypts, overshadowed by ancient trees? An old hospital, with dark corridors filled with antique medical equipment and overturned beds?

Whatever your answer is, you're right. People have their own triggers and their own fears that play into their own personal worst-case scenario. You'd think that a haunted prison would be at the top of the list of places I don't want to hang out in the middle of the night, but for me, that's actually not true. They just don't bother me all that much.

I've definitely investigated a lot of jails where I've seen plenty of activity. I've even spent the night in a cell on Alcatraz. Despite its reputation, that place is one of the least haunted "haunted" locations I've ever visited. We investigated there on *Ghost Hunters*, but my first time was with a group of friends who had all entered into the lottery to get one of the rare and coveted overnight stays on the Rock. We got some interesting EVPs in the morgue, and there was a solitary confinement cell that had a lot of activity in it, but I remember being disappointed that, after all the legends around the supposedly inescapable prison, it wasn't more haunted.

It's easy to assume, given the grim nature of a prison, that they're all haunted and have dark energy around them. The simple truth is that not all of them are like that. Some, like Missouri State Penitentiary, have bloody histories and are very haunted, though.

I've seen a lot of activity in prisons, but most of that activity has not been what you would assume when you hear "I talked to a ghost in a prison." I think people tend to walk into a jail with a preconceived notion of who they're going to meet in spirit form. We really have no idea who we're going to communicate with in there, and we can't know why a person was incarcerated or how they ended up there. I always tell people to abandon all

judgment when they go into a jail, and really just go in
with the human side in mind. Some of these people had
terrible childhoods and made mistakes. A lot of them had
drug problems or were abused. With older prisons, you
could be dealing with someone who was incarcerated for
not being able to pay a one-dollar tax bill. It's not always
going to be a crazy murderer with some really juicy
story to tell.

But again, that could be my intention or my cognitive
bias. I'm sure many people have investigated grim old halls
of incarceration and found much darker evidence and had
scarier experiences. Maybe I'm drawing the human side
out of these ghosts by trying to empathize with them. That
being said, I find that a lot of the spirits that I meet in
jails feel like they belong there—as though they've chosen
to stay behind in a self-imposed sentence. The ghosts I've
found in these places, on the whole, aren't mean. They're
sad. That's why I don't generally feel in danger of getting
attacked in an old prison, and I haven't been (with the exception of the time I was grabbed in Gettysburg, and a few
things being thrown here and there). Those spirits that I've
communicated with aren't even looking for help. They're
just like, *This is where I belong, so I'm staying.* It's almost as
though they feel they don't deserve to move on.

When we investigated the Old St. Johns County Jail
in St. Augustine, Florida, in Season 4 of *Kindred Spirits,*
we knew walking in that the jail had a lot of activity.

Founded in 1655, St. Augustine is the oldest continuously occupied city in America, and that jail had a lot of dark history, having housed prisoners for over one hundred years in inhumane conditions. Disease was rampant in the overcrowded cells, and prisoners fought with and killed each other. The men were forced to work on brutal chain gangs, the members of which were called "the product" in the county's moneymaking scheme to use them for cheap labor. When prisoners were sentenced to death, they were required to build their own gallows, and hundreds of people would come and watch those men be publicly hanged.

"Energy like that doesn't just leave because you've dragged the bodies out," Stephen, general manager of the jail museum, said. He reported that his staff experienced being grabbed and seeing a crawling dark entity. Stephen himself has been nearly pushed down the stairs, in what he felt was a deliberate way.

The corruption at the prison also meant that some innocent men were imprisoned falsely, and were not able to prove their innocence in life. That's what we encountered as soon as we started investigating on the first night.

"Is there anybody here, sheriff, deputy, murderer, outlaw, whoever," Adam said on an EVP session. *I'm not a murderer*, was the response we got back. We immediately knew that was the work we were meant to do in the jail—

but the responses were minimal until I asked, "What was the sheriff's name when you were here? Was he a good sheriff?"

NO, we heard, in the most forceful answer of the night.

The next day we did some research into men imprisoned in that jail who may have been innocent but were still convicted of murder. One case stood out to us: Jim Kirby and Robert Lee were accused of murder, and both were convicted and hanged in 1901. Even though Kirby was adamant that Lee had nothing to do with the crime, he was not exonerated. On the day of the hangings, both men proclaimed Lee's innocence. "They are hanging an innocent man," he said in an article from the *St. Augustine Record* on the day of the hanging. "As God is my Judge and knowing that I must face Him innocent or guilty in a few minutes, I am innocent."

In the same article, Kirby said, "I have tried to save Lee but failed. But you can state that he knew nothing of the affair until it was over."

That night, we asked Chip to do a reading of the solitary confinement cell, which has been an active spot in the jail. He was immediately overwhelmed by emotion. "Whatever I'm picking up says, *I just don't give a damn anymore. No need to even try,*" he said. "It's horrible. Just hopeless. It comes in waves. You don't even feel like there's any reason to exist."

We asked Chip many times if he wanted to leave the

space, but he wanted to finish his reading. "It was horrifying," he said later. "I sat in the chair and I felt such anger and pain. I was frightened, upset, confused, hopeless, helpless—all of those things. I started to shake and I was yelling 'Let me out of here!'" But it was the prisoners he was channeling, and not Chip himself, who were saying those things. "Chip came through and said 'No, I don't need to leave' but whoever I tapped into, it was just horrifying," because of all those negative emotions.

"We're there to help the living and the dead," he said afterward. "Maybe there are people who are still experiencing that upset. Maybe there had been people who were not guilty who were put in that space, or who were mistreated or abused, and they took that with them beyond the grave. It's so complex and so complicated when you start dealing with this stuff. It can be very extreme. Sometimes it can be that extreme."

We eventually made contact with both men, with the help of a staff member of the jail who had had some strong experiences in the space, and told them that we knew the truth about what happened and that we would make sure people knew the real story. Our hope is that by telling the story, and assuring these men that history has set the record straight on what happened, that they'll feel as though they deserve to leave that place, and their work is done.

I feel like people look at old jails as full of evil, but I

still view them as places where people need help—even if it's hard to get them to talk about it. Even when people are alive in prison, there are still people trying to help the incarcerated. I go into any place with that same mindset, whether that's a jail or a mental institution or a hospital. When I enter, I always say I'm not there to judge; I'm not there to tell you what to do. I'm not the police or a doctor. I'm just here to talk.

Maybe it's my maternal nature, but I tend to have the most emotional trouble with places where people were sick and suffering. Inside the Old South Pittsburg Hospital in South Pittsburg, Tennessee, I was alone in the "body box," where corpses would be stored, doing a spirit box session. I was saying words like *who am I?* and *murder*, when something stroked the side of my head in a very creepy way. I had to get out of there. I very much did not like that feeling.

One of the hardest moments I've ever had as an investigator was when Adam and I returned to Waverly Hills Sanatorium in Season 3 of *Kindred*. There are over five hundred rooms across 180,000 square feet in that building, but owner Tina Mattingly asked us back because she was getting a lot of activity that was scaring her and other investigators on the fourth floor of the hospital, in what used to be used as a unit for mental patients.

We started our investigation in that spot with EVP work. "Do you want us to find your family? And if you wouldn't, if you don't want us to find your family and friends, if you just want to talk to us, that's okay too," I said.

The answer came so forcefully that Adam and I both jumped. *NOOOOO.* And it happened in the same spot where Tina had reported screaming in her ear.

We couldn't tell if that man didn't want us to find his family, or if he was saying that he didn't want to talk to us. Once Chip came in, he said that he found "frenzied people saying they don't want to be bothered anymore."

We picked up a lot of hostility and anger, but we were having trouble narrowing down who was so angry or how we could help. In our research the next day, we found a terrible story of a patient at Waverly Hills who had suffered unimaginable personal losses. John Mitchell was at the hospital, ill with tuberculosis, while his wife was home caring for their seven children. She was also having an affair with another man. At 3 a.m. in a café, her lover slapped her so hard that she sustained severe head trauma and died. She was found in an alley the next day, her official cause of death a cerebral hemorrhage caused by a blow to the head. (The man who hit her was found not guilty of murder, but years later, his then-wife died the same way. He was found guilty that time.)

Sick enough to be treated intermittently at Waverly Hills for the past three years, John Mitchell had no choice but to ask the state to care for his kids. He returned to the sanatorium and died. We don't know if he ever even saw them again, or what happened to those kids.

Think about what that would feel like, to be terminally ill, to be betrayed by your wife, to lose her in that traumatic way, and to be forced by those circumstances to willingly surrender your kids to the state.

Of course he would be angry. And of course he would feel like he had reason to stay behind.

Once we thought we were speaking to John Mitchell, we returned to that spot on the fourth floor to investigate, but whoever was already there did not want us to be there. Adam's SLS camera turned off four times, even though it was fully charged. Eventually, frustrated, Adam gave up on that equipment, and we relied only on our recorder.

"My question to you is, are you or do you know who John Mitchell is?" I asked.

Mitchell, he said.

"Do you feel like your life was taken from you?"

YES.

It was so strong. All of a sudden, a breeze picked up out of nowhere, only in that one hallway. It became strangely windy for just a minute. Then we heard footsteps coming from the hallway.

"John, if that's you, we want nothing but the best for you," I said. "We don't want you to be here—"

Just then, something appeared in the hallway.

It was a man.

A full-bodied apparition was standing directly in front of us.

It appeared out of nowhere, and disappeared in a flash.

It was not a shadow figure. It was a person.

I hadn't seen anything like that since I was a kid. That was horror-movie level. I was legitimately terrified.

"That shit is rare," Adam said. "It is so rare." As we listened to the recording, I jumped, then said to Adam, "Oh, that was you. You touched me."

"I didn't," he said. "I was over here the whole time."

It was the strongest and clearest encounter with a ghost I've had in decades.

We think John Mitchell appeared that way because we identified him by name—maybe for the first time since he'd died—and because we knew he had been through something unimaginably bad. When he showed himself, it was almost like he was trying to say, *I'm here, you're right, now leave me alone.*

The next day when we talked to Tina, we told her about John and his story. "We recommend when you have investigators come in," I said, "you make them aware of him, so the more they talk to him—"

"Maybe he can let go," Tina said. "I'll try to help him."

"That wasn't our focus when we came in, but it became that," Adam said.

"Well they made sure that that was your focus," Tina answered, referring to the many spirits in the space.

They probably knew he needed it most.

That time in Waverly Hills, I really was terrified. But that is a rare exception, especially these days. People often ask me why I react so strongly when we get a big piece of evidence on the show. In general, I might look scared, but I'm really excited. Imagine sitting in the dark for four hours, hoping something's going to happen, and then it finally does. You'd be pretty excited, too, even if it was just a recording of someone saying, *Go away.*

I'm infrequently afraid when I'm investigating. There are definitely moments when I get creeped out, but it's more like wonderment and excitement. I will get an adrenaline rush for a minute, but then I launch into research-and-analysis mode. I want to figure out the "why."

"Once you have a job to do, that mechanism clicks off. You click off the terror switch because you can't be terrified," Adam said. "I think it just naturally occurs when you give yourself a purpose with ghosts. We get a little freaked out at times, but that's fun. When you have purpose and focus, the fear pushes to the side because what you're doing is more important. Finding the answers is more important than being affected by the scare factor."

There are exceptions, though, like at Waverly Hills. Once, when Kris Williams and I were investigating a home on *Ghost Hunters* and while we were in the middle of the pitch-black basement, a deep, gravelly voice said

HELP ME right in between us. We both jumped out of our skins. But even then, that was more like getting startled than genuinely being terrified. That's only happened a handful of times.

When there's a train coming that's going to run me over, that's scary, too.

Even if it's a ghost train.

When we visited the Crocker Tavern House in Barnstable, Massachusetts, on Season 3 of *Kindred Spirits*, we went there to investigate activity that had been happening over the past year to the home's new owners. The building was erected in 1754 as a stagecoach stop and tavern, but then became a museum and eventually a residential home. With over 250 years of history, the house had accumulated a lot of stories. Kate and her husband, Joe, saw a dark shadow running toward their baby. Other family members heard footsteps, and some even claimed to have been locked in a room by what they felt was a ghost.

Early in our investigation, we got the name Willie on an EVP. Then later in our research, we learned a lot more about who that person might be. In 1926, there was a terrible accident not far from the house. A train had struck a car. Two women died on the scene, and another died at the hospital. Among them: Wilhelmina Crocker.

"Was there a car accident?" Adam asked in a spirit box experiment that night.

Hurry.

"Hurry and do what?"

Where are you going?

"Are you part of a family that lives here?"

Other one.

From speaking to a Crocker family historian, we had learned that a Wilhelmina Jones had lived next door to the house and had married into the Crocker family. It would make sense that she would return to this house, because it looks familiar to her. It has stayed nearly exactly the same in the century since her accident.

To communicate with Wilhelmina, we decided to try something we'd never done before: to attempt to record activity in the home she was haunting by using the site of her death as a trigger object.

I drove to the train tracks, and Adam stayed in the house. The idea was that I would do EVP work at the tracks, while he listened to the spirit box at the house for responses. We couldn't hear the other's work and had no way of knowing what the other person was doing.

"Amy is out there by the train tracks," Adam said. "Is she safe out there? They don't have anyone there signaling cars to stop when the train is coming, so it's really scary." After he said that, he moved to another room— as he walked past, a lamp in the hallway blinked off and on in an intense pattern. Was Wilhelmina trying to communicate?

"Hello? I know there was a terrible accident and I feel like one of you might be looking for help," I said at the tracks. "My friend is at the Crocker Tavern right now. He's waiting for you."

At the same time, Adam heard in the spirit box: *Hi, I'm outside.*

"Why did you go there?" I asked. "Who was there who could help you?"

Help me, Adam heard. Then a scream in the spirit box.

"Can you say something if you're here?" I asked. "Just talk into this little red light, or go see my friend at the Crocker Tavern, his name is Adam."

Adam heard an explosion.

There was definitely something there with me. I didn't know if it was residual energy from the accident, but I didn't like it one bit.

Just then, the lights and bells went off, as though a train were coming.

I nearly jumped out of my skin.

The crew and I ran toward the car, but I wanted to see if there really was a train coming. We waited.

Nothing.

That was it for me. I was done. I was shaking. Had Wilhelmina set off that alarm? Was she trying to warn me of something?

Although it scared me half to death, the experiment was successful. Adam was hearing responses to the questions I was asking. Back at the house, after Adam and I compared evidence, we decided to talk to Willie again.

"I went to the train tracks where you were killed," I ventured in an EVP session. "Did you see me there?"

Yes.

"Can you tell us who Clarence Shirley Crocker is?"

My husband.

"It's almost a hundred years since you passed away."

No.

We were stunned. She didn't know she had died. I can't imagine spending almost a hundred years in a place, not knowing what was happening to you, or why. We had to tell her the truth.

"Can you read this? I'm just bringing it here to show you that it's your death certificate."

Death certificate?

"Tell us what you want us to do."

I'm going home.

"Mrs. Crocker, I know this is hard, but we'll make sure no one forgets you, okay?"

With that, silence.

When we spoke to Kate and Joe the next day, she told us that trains didn't even run on Cape Cod in the middle of winter. There was no way that train signal went off for an actual train.

Since we visited, they've experienced smaller instances of activity—you can accumulate a lot of ghosts in two and a half centuries—but nothing on the scale of the activity that had been happening previously, and nothing that scares them anymore. We hope Willie really did, as she said, go home.

THE GHOST AND THE SHOWRUNNER

You might think seeing John Mitchell appear at Waverly Hills was the biggest thing that happened that night—but you'd be wrong. While that was going on, our former showrunner Brian Garrity was having his own experience, and we had no idea.

In the middle of our spirit box session, Brian started having a massive coughing attack from all of the dust and dirt in the old building. We stopped filming so he could have some time to recover, but he was having a really hard time breathing. Eventually he told us to start again, but he was still struggling to breathe, and doing everything he could do to stay silent. But we were getting so much crazy activity that he couldn't stop what he was doing, which was to write down the evidence we were getting as we were getting it.

So we're picking up all these responses, and we have no idea why we keep hearing *Help him, help him.* But Brian knows, because he can't breathe as he's writing down that the ghosts are telling us our friend needs assistance.

Just then, he felt a strong hand on his back, almost as though someone was trying to help him stop coughing. Waverly Hills had been a tuberculosis hospital. The spirits there had seen that kind of episode many times.

Maybe that's why we were able to isolate John Mitchell after all—because the other spirits there were preoccupied with trying to help our friend.

Chapter 10

IF GHOSTS ARE REAL, BIGFOOT IS PROBABLY REAL TOO

AT STRANGE ESCAPES events, John Tenney always starts his lectures by asking three questions.

"How many people here believe in ghosts?" he asks. Everyone in the room, for the most part, raises their hands.

"Okay, and how many people here believe in aliens?" Slightly fewer people raise their hands.

"And then, how many people here believe in Bigfoot?" Only a few hands are raised.

The reason he asks, he explains, is that one of the things he's interested in as a researcher is why people believe the things they believe. "So the first question I ask is, do you believe in ghosts? Do you believe that there's a persistence and consciousness and personality that exists beyond the biological realm? And the majority of you said yes," he said at our most recent event at the Mount Washington Hotel. "And then I said, do you believe in aliens? Do you think that life has arisen, developed, evolved, developed technology, traversed the inky blackness of the infinitude of the cosmos and found us here on this tiny little backwater planet in the middle of the galaxy? And most of you said yes.

"And I said, do you believe that there's an animal we haven't discovered?" he continued. "And people shrugged their shoulders and laughed, *No, that's ridiculous.* That third one is the most possible of the three and it's the one that people find the most ridiculous."

The answers, in that ratio, are the same every time he poses those questions at a Strange Escapes event. It never surprises me, but it does always baffle me. Why, if you're so open to and interested in one paranormal phenomenon that you traveled to a weekend event to learn more about it, does the idea that there are other plausible paranormal phenomena out there sound so unlikely? Until a few years ago, I would have probably given the same answers the majority of the group did—but now that I've started looking outside the strictly drawn lines of ghost research, I've seen so many interesting connections and ideas to consider.

I'm not just saying that because I've seen Andrea Perron,

the eldest daughter from the family who inspired *The Conjuring*, call UFOs down from the sky. Going by John's poll numbers above, slightly less than half of you are probably calling bullshit on that statement right now— but I assure you that I have, in fact, witnessed it, and it is exactly as freaky as it seems. Andrea and I, and a few other people, went out on the deck of the *Queen Mary*, and she started singing to the sky. All of a sudden, in the middle of a thick fog where no stars were visible at all, there were little streaks of light everywhere. I hightailed it back inside. I may not be afraid of ghosts, but aliens chill me to my bones.

The thing is, and I will keep saying this until I'm a ghost myself: There is no right answer when it comes to the paranormal. There is no definitive guide to which parts are right, and which parts are wrong, and which things we're calling ghosts are really part of the animal world, or which parts of life on Earth are not actually from this planet at all. I've read theories before that Bigfoot is the ghost of a Neanderthal, and that the Loch Ness Monster is the ghost of a dinosaur.

Maybe that sounds crazy to you, but really, who's to say for sure that those theories are wrong? If you believe that in order to become a ghost, you have to have a soul, does that automatically exclude every living thing that isn't human from potential ghostliness? We can't say for sure that animals do or don't have souls—but if you've ever had your dog intuit that you're sad and give you extra love on a day you really need it, you probably already know your own answer to that question. (I've also gotten EVPs of a cat purring while on a home investigation in Keene, New Hampshire, so there's that, too.)

The same goes for humanoids who lived before Homo sapiens. Do we know for sure that those beings *didn't* become ghosts? Put the soul question aside for a second and think about what other characteristics might be necessary for something to have the potential to become a ghost. Maybe those required factors are intelligence, consciousness, and self-awareness. As far as we know, humanoids before us had these qualities. So to me, it's just as plausible that Neanderthals became ghosts the same way humans do.

Then again, maybe that's because I'm pretty sure I saw a yeti when I was a kid.

When I was around ten years old and living in Petaluma, California, my siblings and our friends would spend our days exploring the woods around our house. Our parents were basically like, *Go play, and don't come back until it's dark.* Remember how you could do that in the eighties and it was totally fine?

One night, it was dusk, and we were running through a field across the street from my house. I knew this field like the back of my hand: The grass and vegetation were so tall they grew above our heads, and there was a dry creek bed we would follow that put us up on a little hill. From there, we could see the forest, and a taller hill beyond. As we crested the hill, we all stopped in our tracks.

There was a huge creature in front of us. It was maybe eight feet tall, and so white that it was almost transparent. And it was coming down the next hill toward us.

None of us said a word. We turned and ran as fast as we could—the most panicked fleeing you can imagine—until we got back to the house. "What was that?" I asked when I could breathe again. My brother responded, "I don't know what it was."

I know what you're thinking. Every time I tell this story, I feel exactly as nutty as I sound.

It was one of those things that scared us so deeply we never spoke about it again. Fast-forward five or six years later, and I was in high school, hanging out at this concert venue in Petaluma called the Phoenix Theater. (That place is so haunted that AFI wrote a song about the spirits in the theater, and a security guard for GWAR once reportedly saw a little ghost boy backstage. I've investigated it many times.) I would go there with all the other wayward misfits who wanted a place to hang out after school, and the manager would keep it open in the afternoons to give us a safe place to be.

One day around dusk, I was standing outside with my friends, and this kid we knew came barreling down the sidewalk, sweating and panting. He couldn't even talk.

Eventually he told us that he had come from the forest by the graveyard—the one near my house—and that he had seen this big, weird, white creature. I had never told anyone about what we'd seen five years ago. My brother definitely didn't know that kid, and the friends who had been there with us that day had long since moved away. His description, though, was exactly what I had encountered years before.

I had chills just remembering that creature. My friends wanted to go back and see it. Even though I didn't want to, I went. We hopped the fence into the graveyard and took the shortcut to the other side of the forest. The whole twenty minutes we were walking, the kid didn't budge on what he saw. He kept repeating the same thing, and he was clearly agitated. But when we got closer, he said he couldn't go through with going back. He was too scared, and he ran home.

We kept going, back to the place where he had come across whatever he had spotted. We heard loud footsteps—they'd come from one side of us, and then from the other, way too quickly for someone to have made it back and forth without detection—but we didn't see the creature. Years and years later, Greg and Dana Newkirk would give a talk at the Mount Washington about their theories on how Bigfoot is an interdimensional being. Was he popping in and out of that forest that day? Who knows?

To me, there's too much intersection between different

fields of paranormal study to be able to pick and choose that some are real and some are not. I've seen too much overlap to say definitively that only ghosts exist and nothing else does. Remember that investigation in Pennsylvania where the homeowner Catherine's son, who had died in infancy, was appearing as thirty-three years old in her home? Catherine also told us things that sounded eerily like an alien abduction. It didn't make it to air, but she said that on a few occasions, she woke up to something in her house that looked like a big sphere of light, with two crystals coming out from underneath the sphere. Her house was definitely haunted, but it seemed like there was something else going on there, too.

I've heard a lot of stories about hauntings that sound to me like they could be alien experiences, or sound like they have elements of other phenomena associated with them. This is why I don't believe there are strict lines between disciplines. I think the world is more connected than we know—and because of that, I don't think you can believe in one and completely discount the other. There are so many things that are strikingly similar. If you have a mind that's open enough to believe in ghosts, why would you not believe in something like a cryptid (an unproven creature like Bigfoot) or the idea of UFOs? To me, aliens are so much more plausible than ghosts. Even though I believe in them and I study them, if I were going to pick one thing that absolutely existed, I would definitely choose life on another planet coming to see us.

I feel the same way about psychic ability, as many people doubt it exists. You're telling me you believe in ghosts, but you're not going to believe in the idea that someone could have some kind of enhanced mental ability? That's hard for me to wrap my head around.

"The first paper that was ever written about orbs was actually written by a guy named Bruce Maccabee," John said in that same lecture. Maccabee was a UFO researcher and an optical physicist. "When digital cameras came around, UFO researchers started to see orbs all the time. He was the first one who wrote about particulate matter and dog hair and dust and how you can re-create orbs."

Just like orbs were first tied to aliens, the same goes with spirit boxes. Frank Sumption made those first Frank's Boxes to communicate with aliens. In fact, he said he was given the specs for the first prototype by aliens themselves. Years ago, at the Stanley, I spent time with Frank during a few paranormal events. He was always tickled that paranormal investigators had taken such a liking to his inventions. Frank refused to charge for them, and he only gave them to people he trusted, so that's why there are so few of them out there in the world.

One night, he was demonstrating the boxes to a group of us in one of the smaller bedrooms. All of a sudden, the box kept saying my name over and over. *Amy, Amy, Amy.*

Frank looked up at me and said, "See? They like you." I don't know whether it was ghosts or aliens, but something seemed excited to see me.

"If you pigeonhole yourself, and only focus on one thing without looking at the bigger narrative, you might miss the commonalities and the threads between these different aspects of the supernatural that could open up new paradigms and discussion points," Greg Newkirk said. He and Dana take a multidisciplinary approach to their investigations, and often apply knowledge from various areas of study to one case. Their show *Hellier* begins as a paranormal investigation for goblins and becomes a larger search for aliens and, eventually, ancient gods.

"People start to get ingrained in their own version of weirdness," he added. "The ghost hunters don't want to talk about aliens. In reality, it's all probably just different names for the same type of thing. You can call them ghosts, you can call them demons, call them aliens, Bigfoot, whatever you want."

The Newkirks developed their particular brand of interconnective thinking from time spent with people who believe they have been abducted by aliens or who believe they have seen cryptids. "As we investigated ghosts, we realized how valuable it was to hang out with these people who believe they were abducted by aliens," Greg said. "There's so much crossover that's not getting discussed because these separate areas of people studying the phenomena won't come together and talk about it. So it became our obsession to figure out what was overlapping. Are people looking into UFOs experiencing the same types of things that people are when exploring haunted places? Where is the crossover, and how can we correlate it?"

What makes the difference in what an investigator discovers all has to do with cognitive bias. What you are looking for is what you're going to find. "The variable factors mainly fall into two important areas," said Loren Coleman, a leading scholar of cryptozoology. "Those who are experiencing the phenomena and those who are investigating it. Depending on the participants' background, point of view, and perceived reflective experiences, a noise in the woods could be felt to be—in the extreme—an unknown cryptid (like Bigfoot, a mystery cat, Dogman, etc.), a ghost or demon, or a serial killer.

"That's where the investigator's role and biases come into play," Loren added. "The much more strongly specialized the researcher, the more directed an investigation will result." Someone looking at a structure of unknown origin, he explained, will look toward their own area of interest for an explanation. "Someone who is a ufologist might look at that site and wonder if aliens made it. A maverick archaeologist could consider Viking or megalithic explorers. Someone else could discuss Freemasons and the Illuminati."

The Newkirks, though, see more connections in those areas than they do divisions. "There's something much bigger and weirder than just a big, hairy ape or an extra-terrestrial or a ghost," Greg said. "The point—what we're trying to do—is figure out the source of that. I think it has to do with the mind."

"Our goal is always to remind people that those experiences you're having are legitimate experiences," Dana said. "We might not have answers for them right now, but that doesn't take away from the fact that you've legitimately experienced something that's bizarre. Instead of being afraid of those things or being ashamed of those things, the more we can reinvent the world and the more we can bring back wonder, the more we'll look at those experiences as being beautiful and positive rather than scary or evil or not real."

THE DARKEST CORNERS OF THE *QUEEN MARY*

Nowadays, the *Queen Mary* so fully embraces its haunted legacy that the ship offers ghost tours, and even hosts creepy Halloween events deep beneath the waterline, in the boiler room.

That was not always the case, though.

Back in my early days as an investigator, I was helping with a paranormal event on the ship. I was down in the boiler room with Britt Griffith, my first investigating partner, checking out the space for people to potentially investigate later on. Today, the cavernous space has been redone. There are fully lit walking tours of the inner workings of the ship, but under investigating conditions, the boiler room has just enough lighting to illuminate the elevated walkways and still feel appropriately creepy.

Back then, it was dark, decrepit, and downright terrifying.

At one point, we both looked over in the same direction, and even in the dim glow of our flashlights, we both saw another man down there with us in the boiler room.

But it wasn't a whole man.

I could see he was wearing some kind of work outfit, like overalls, and I could see his arm, his torso, and part of his head. It was definitely a ghost, but it was only part of a ghost.

I grabbed Britt. "What did I just see?" I said. "Did

you see that?" He did. We compared notes, and we saw the same thing.

A year or more later, I found out that there was a ghost in that space named Henry. He worked in the boiler room, and his remains were reportedly found in the bottom of the ship's hull. The free-floating half torso and half head of the man are sometimes seen in that space. Some people speculate that Henry appears that way because of an injury, but it could just also be that he doesn't have enough energy to appear as a full-bodied man. Or maybe he just doesn't want to. We can't be sure which.

Chapter 11

IT TAKES A (HAUNTED) VILLAGE

YOU MIGHT HAVE noticed that, for something I wrote, this book contains a good amount of information from other experts. That's because, in my view, I can't do my best work alone. Working in and with the larger community, especially the people pushing the boundaries of traditional investigating methods, has had a profound impact on me, not just in the way I investigate on the show, but in the way I think about the paranormal as a whole.

There have been so many times when someone else's input, or their knowledge of a specialized subject, has been the key to unlocking the case. (See also: Dana Newkirk's tarot card reading in Connecticut in Chapter 7;

John Tenney's superhuman research skills at the Odd Fellows Home at Belvoir Winery in Chapter 6; Chip Coffey's psychic ability in, oh, every case we've ever asked him to participate in.)

In cases on the show, and at Strange Escapes events, it's really important to me to include other experts on the subject. I feel more voices only enhance the experience for everyone, including myself. I love to hear about other people's cases, and the creative ways they approached their investigations. It's just as fun for me to listen to their perspectives as it is for everyone else there. Even if you've never gone on an investigation before, just think about how much different the experience would be if you were to go to a haunted house or an escape room alone versus with a group of friends. It would be fun by yourself, but it would be a lot more fun if you had people to go through it with you, and with whom you could talk about it afterward.

"I'm going to try and throw some weird seeds into your brain and start growing new thoughts about phenomena and the ideas that you already have," John said at his lecture at the Mount Washington. "I just want to make a more well-informed, stranger, weirder community. That way you can think about weird things and bring them back to me and we can discuss and construct ideas that we couldn't have done alone."

So, it really does take a village—albeit, a haunted

one—to do the kind of work I want to do. Collaboration is key if we want to move the conversation forward about the paranormal, and come up with outside-the-box ways of learning more about a challenging and sometimes controversial topic.

In October 2019, the *Kindred Spirits* cast participated in *Haunted Salem: Live*, broadcast on Travel Channel. During this live televised event, three paranormal teams from different shows on the network collaborated to have a huge investigation of the town of Salem, Massachusetts, where the Salem Witch Trials of 1692 saw more than two hundred people accused of witchcraft, nineteen of them hanged and one, Giles Corey, pressed to death under a pile of rocks. Adam, Chip, and I investigated the John Proctor House, the former home of one of the men falsely accused of witchcraft and executed. The cast of *Ghost Brothers* investigated the old town jail where Giles Corey had been imprisoned, and the cast of *Portals to Hell* investigated a haunted restaurant that sits atop the site of a former church where the accused were excommunicated before they were hanged.

Rather than just investigate the John Proctor House, though, Adam and I wanted to do something we had never done before—let alone seen on television. We had Greg and Dana Newkirk join us at the house, to attempt an intention experiment that paired magic rituals with paranormal investigation, and we tapped into the viewers at home to help us pull it off. Pretty cool, right? And we haven't even gotten to the part about the haunted tarot deck yet.

An intention experiment, in its simplest form, just involves a group of people focusing their minds on one specific outcome and observing what happens. There's a lot of talk about whether they actually work, but to me, it's all speculation. We cannot measure intention as it relates to outcome, but I have observed so many interesting things when a group of people get together and put their minds toward something.

So when we have a big group of paranormal enthusiasts together, it's an opportunity to hold a semi-controlled intention experiment and observe the results. It's not scientific—there isn't a way to measure intention scientifically—but it's still interesting to see what happens. For example, on a Strange Escapes at Sea event, we were cruising through the Bermuda Triangle, and we brought everyone who wanted to participate out on deck for an experiment led by John and Dana. (It says a lot about our cast of characters that while most people would be freaked out sailing through a legendarily dangerous place, almost every Escapee was like "Yeah! Let's do weird stuff in the Triangle!")

It was a cloudy night, and the water was calm. When everyone was out on deck, Dana gave each person a crystal to help focus their intention, and John had people quietly focus on what had been holding them back in their lives. "Envision it as a bright star," he said, "and throw it out to sea."

At that moment, the clouds parted, the moon shone down on the group, and "in a matter of moments," John said, "the boat was covered in these really beautiful, colorful dragonflies." Over the next few days, people on the cruise who weren't even part of our group, and so would have no idea what we had been doing, commented on the moment the dragonflies overtook the boat. A lot more people than just Escapees witnessed it happen.

The thing is, we were *way* too far out to sea for dragonflies to have been able to reach us from land. When we got back to port, we all started researching dragonflies, trying to figure out whether we had wandered into a migration path. What we found out was that dragonflies didn't migrate at that time of year, and they don't swarm over open ocean. There was no reasonable explanation for what happened.

"Dragonflies are a reminder of change and growth," John said. "These tiny bugs that grow at the bottom of ponds can become these beautiful, translucent creatures. It was a way to show people that change happens, and they wanted to be part of that experience."

The dragonfly phenomena is not the only time something unexplainable like that has happened, not by a mile.

We've had some really beautiful experiences on Strange Escapes in Hawaii, where local guide "Uncle" Joe Espinda Jr., has taken us out on hikes to sacred sites. He has performed rituals with chants and prayers, and led us in meditations. I can't speak to anyone else's personal feelings, but those moments resulted in enlightening, spiritual experiences for me, when I felt at one with the island and that I was tapping into energies bigger than myself.

With *Haunted Salem*, we had the opportunity to connect in real time with our biggest group yet of people curious about the paranormal, and we wanted to do something particularly unique and special. Greg and Dana suggested an intention experiment for the five of us to participate in (the other three being me, Adam, and Chip) where Dana would perform some magic rituals while Greg painted a sigil that would function as a kind of door to the other side. The energy and intentions of the viewers at home would amplify our energy and add to the power of our investigation. Since this was happening in one of the places most intimately associated with witchcraft in the world, we felt that bringing magic into the night could be extraordinarily meaningful.

First, Dana cast a witch's circle, a consecrated space to raise and contain energy. She told us to visualize a bubble around the room, while she said, "Earth is my body, air is my breath, fire is my spirit, water is my blood. I cast the circle in perfect love and perfect trust.

So mote it be." Once the circle was cast, we were in that room until the ritual was over. The circle also functioned as protection for us, to prevent anything negative from entering the space.

Then Greg started to paint the sigil, using consecrated ink. "This symbol is going to be a portable doorway to the dead," he said. The sigil was created with the specific intention. "This space is a door for the dead," he said, and he painted using those consonants to represent the intention. The magical symbol would help us connect to and communicate with the spirit world, but we needed help to power the symbol—so we asked viewers at home to concentrate on the sigil, to focus all their energy and intention on it, to even draw it at home if they wanted to.

While this was happening, I did a spirit box experiment with an original Frank's Box. The energy in the room was so high that I was already feeling antsy, but I started. Even before anyone asked me a question, I heard, *Hi.*

"Who's here with us?" Adam asked.

My family.

"How many of you are here?" Adam said.

Chip asked, "What's your name?"

I can't hear you.

When I said that, Adam spoke to the viewers at home: "Everybody focus on the door, focus on opening the door."

"Does this symbol bother you?" Chip asked.

Bring me home. Go away.

"I'm sorry but we're going to be here for a while," Adam said. "Can you tell us your name? Are you Giles Corey?"

My kids.

"Are you John Proctor? Elizabeth?"

Knife.

Chip asked, "Who used a knife?"

Making money off of death.

"Were you accused of being a witch?"

The attic.

"Can you just tell us how old you are?" Adam asked. "Are you a child?"

It's there.

"Okay, but who's there? What's there?"

The people. Attic.

As this was happening, James McDaniel, who was reporting on social media responses during the broadcast, said that responses to the sigil were significant. "People all across the nation right now are reporting headaches, tightness in their chests, people smelling smoke, saying it's coming from their concentration on the sigil," he said. He quoted someone saying, "I have never felt so affected by something on TV." It got so intense that producers asked Dave Schrader, who was cohosting the broadcast, to interject at one point and tell people how to close the sigil—by turning it upside down—so they could control the energy in their homes.

The energy in the house was palpable. We could all feel it buzzing around us, and the temperature in the room had dropped dramatically. Dana broke the circle. "Think about it in terms of a dam," she said. "All the energy that we've built up in this space is going to flow through the house."

We went and investigated the attic, but we didn't find the people the spirit I was channeling kept talking about. So we went back downstairs, and we all sat around the dining room table, hands touching. It was time for Chip to start a séance.

There was so much energy from the experiment we could literally feel the table buzzing underneath us, almost like it was electrified.

"John Proctor, if you're in this space, come and be with us now in this circle," Chip said. "We know that you had a very interesting history in this town. And we want to know more about you, and perhaps correct some of the things that history's told us about you or verify them."

The table was vibrating to the point where it was rocking back and forth. Chip, in trying to tap into the spirits in the house, went blank. "Chip?" I asked. "Are you okay?" He didn't respond. We tried shouting, waving our hands—nothing. It finally took Adam slapping him lightly on the cheek to bring him back to us.

"More weight," Chip said. He was picking up the phrase that Giles Corey repeated over and over while he was being tortured. He was pressed to death under rocks because, unlike the people who were tried and hanged, Corey refused to enter a plea and therefore couldn't be tried. The torture was an attempt to extract a plea from him, not to kill him. Every time the sheriff demanded an answer, Corey would repeat "More weight." After three days of that hell, he died—but some say his last words were, "Damn you. I curse you and Salem!"

So when Chip heard *More weight*, he knew who he was dealing with, and it definitely wasn't John Proctor in his own house. "We may have somebody pretending to be somebody else. Giles Corey. Giles is faking us out."

Every time I closed my eyes, I felt dizzy. "It's completely disorienting in this room, and freezing," Chip said. "Dana, flip another card and see what it's going to tell us."

The first time Dana pulled from the haunted tarot deck, she unveiled The Devil. "It's all about manipulation," she explained. "It's about the kind of people who know they're manipulating, and hurting people, and they don't care. They get enjoyment out of it." Like, possibly, a man who had been so wronged that he cursed an entire town?

Dana shuffled and shuffled the deck. She flipped a card.

For the second time in a row, it was The Devil. There was unquestionably something not nice in that room.

Intention matters a lot in paranormal investigation. In this case, it's unlikely we would have experienced such strong responses if we had not received the help of people at home adding their energy and intention to our work. We feel as though we spoke directly to one of the city's most notorious ghosts, because we set an intention to aim high and make that contact.

The *Haunted Salem: Live* broadcast is the only time we have ever attempted something on that scale before. On Strange Escapes, our experiments have maybe fifty or a hundred people. But the same principle of intention applies to individual investigations, also. When you go into one with a specific outcome or result in mind, you would be surprised at how often you get results in line with the intention you put in. Cognitive bias—that is, seeing only what you want to see—has a lot to do with it, but that's not the whole explanation. "If we're on an Amy Bruni investigation, we know we can probably expect a certain type of activity," Greg said. "But we've done some with people on television shows where they scream at ghosts, and they draw a different crowd, and we have a much different type of activity at that type of investigation. That doesn't mean it's objectively what happened. It just means that's the experience they prompted.

"The way we start pretty much every investigation is by having a little meditation, like a visualization exercise where the only thing that we want to focus on is communication," he added. "I think it's very important before you go in to sit down and do your best to let all that other stuff float away, and just focus on being there for a specific purpose. If you can do that, you're going to have a better experience."

"Some people roll their eyes a little bit," Dana said, "but one of the things we talk about a lot when we're leading group investigations is that your intention going into it will really dictate your experience. When you get groups of people who, for instance, prefer one ghost hunting show over another, and maybe that show has a way of investigating that's a little bit more aggressive or skews a little bit darker, they'll bring that energy with them into the investigation." That energy will often lead to more antagonistic responses, or more anger coming through.

"The thing about the paranormal is it's subjective, and if you want to experience it, you have to subject yourself to it," Greg added. "Only the people who decide to seek it out, or who are in a mental space that seems to attract that type of activity, are going to experience it. You see hauntings in places where there's trauma, abuse, or difficulty and things are in a state of agitation or incompleteness."

Sometimes—and this might sound a little strange—the key to solving what's going on in a case comes from someone who is not experiencing the activity, and who does not even necessarily believe in ghosts. In that case in Connecticut in Chapter 2 where the new homeowners were doing renovations and getting a ton of scary-seeming activity, the problem stemmed from a translation issue. Mr. Kotek, the Polish immigrant who originally owned the house, never learned to speak English—so he quite literally couldn't understand what was going on in his home. We needed the help of a translator to do our job. So we called in a woman to translate for us who worked at a nearby Polish restaurant. She helped us to communicate with him, and together we were all able to help fix the problem.

Once, it was not even a person we needed to help us: It was a band. At the Twisted Vine, a restaurant in Derby, Connecticut, there was a lot of activity. The staff reported seeing apparitions, hearing voices, and having strange things happen with the electronics several times a week. Customers became so creeped out by what they saw and sensed they would often get up and leave. We heard the spirit haunting the restaurant—they called him Sam—would usually appear when he heard music coming from the tavern space downstairs. So, on a Season 4 episode of *Kindred Spirits*, we called in a band, and had them play live while we investigated. Almost immediately, Sam showed up on our SLS camera. That was the first break in helping solve the mystery.

The building, erected in 1892, had been a bank until it was converted into a restaurant in the late 1970s. Mike, the owner of the Twisted Vine, had given us some items associated with the bank. Later on that day, when we used a banknote as a trigger object, Sam told us that he recognized the paperwork. From there, we were able to find a Samuel Lesseey, a longtime employee of what used to be Birmingham National Bank, who took his life in the building in November 1913. Lesseey had been tied to a theft there: A customer had modified a twenty-five-dollar check to pay out $2,500. The shame of the mistake and the ensuing scandal are believed to have led him to commit suicide. He walked to a local cemetery, laid down in a coffin box in a mausoleum, and shot himself in the head. The story spread as far as the West Coast, showing up in the *Los Angeles Herald*, albeit with his name spelled as "Lessep" and "Lessey" in the story.

I also have several stories where people who wouldn't necessarily call themselves believers were key in helping solve a case. But one that stands out was at the Sterling Hill Mine in Ogdensburg, New Jersey. The mine opened in 1630, and was one of the richest veins of zinc ore in the country until it closed in 1986.

Now, the mine is a historical attraction and museum that brings in an estimated twenty-five thousand kids a year on field trips—which is why the tour guides had become so uncomfortable with the strange activity they had been witnessing in the mines of late. Freddy, a tour guide, reported that people were seeing faces in the windows of the museum and hearing voices and footsteps in the mine. One ghost, who he said seemed angry, was pushing people.

The mine, though, was hard to investigate. Because neither Adam nor I had spent much time in abandoned mines before—weird, right?—we had a difficult time discerning normal mine noises from potentially paranormal noises.

One of the things Freddy had mentioned is that when people approached the mine shaft, all the lights would go on at once, but when the person backed away, the lights would go off again. It was almost as if someone was telling people not to go near there, warning them to stay away from a dangerous place.

Freddy experienced so much paranormal activity in and around the mine he couldn't deny it was haunted. Doug, a mine worker who's now a mine historian, was adamant there was no haunting. He had never seen or heard anything, he said, and he worked there for twelve years.

Normally, we rely so much on the slightest sounds for our investigations. In the mine, though, there were so many noises. We needed Doug's help to tell us what was normal, and what might not be. Even though he said he didn't believe in ghosts, he was a good sport about it. Doug put on his mining gear and went underground with us.

There was a rumbling noise we kept hearing, but we couldn't pinpoint it. "That sounds like an ore cart," Doug said. Only the mine wasn't in operation. There were definitely no ore carts moving on the tunnel tracks.

We kept moving through the mine and got to another place where it sounded like there were voices coming from the other end of the tunnel. "What does that sound like to you?" we asked Doug. "It sounds like voices," he said. Another noise that definitely wasn't a normal mine noise. "Twelve years, times fifty-two weeks, times five days a week—I walked in here over three thousand times," he said, "and at the end of the day back out another three thousand times."

"And yet you've never heard the voices you heard tonight until now," I said.

"True," he said, "that's true."

Off camera, Doug said, "I honestly never sat still here. Every time I've been in this mine, I've been working. There are other men working. It's always loud." He seemed truly perplexed at what he was witnessing. I could tell he was opening up his mind to the idea that there was something otherworldly happening there.

We started looking into deaths in the mine, and we learned nearly two hundred people had died from accidents and explosions throughout its history. I took information from a few, including a railway collision that killed three men in 1909, and an accident one of the workers had inadvertently caused when he stepped out of the cage that brought men down the mine shaft, and the cage crashed down another five hundred feet, killing the other two men inside.

"Hi, my name is Amy, thank you for talking with us to-night," I said in a spirit box experiment that evening. "My friend Adam here should be able to hear your answers, so just talk as loud as you can. We're just trying to figure out who is still here, and why."

There's a crowd.

"Do you know about the cars that crashed here? This was in 1909. Three men died." Nothing. "Did you know about the elevator accident?"

An audible gasp from Adam. He asked, "Is there some-body standing right here?" There wasn't.

I was chased out.

"Chased out of the mines?"

Out of the mine.

"Okay, who chased you out of the mine? Were you chased out from your job?"

I was out of work.

"Was your job something to do with the cage?"

Operational.

"Did you cause an accident?"

Come on now.

"Did something happen where you were treated un-fairly?"

I can't describe it.

"Did you do something wrong? Did you not follow a procedure?"

I apologize.

It seemed like someone did something that resulted in an accident, and this ghost felt bad about it. As we discussed it, the lamp in front of us went out completely. I turned it back on.

Once we knew whoever we were talking to was tied to that cage accident, we went back down into the mine, and brought Chip with us. He immediately got a read on the situation, that someone there was feeling "so defensive that he's almost aggressive." This lined up with the angry ghost who was scaring people, and trying to get them to leave by shutting off the lights.

Then, of course, all the lights in the mine went off. While we were alone down there.

"Can you tell us your name?" Adam asked in an EVP session.

Carroll, Frank.

So this was the man who caused the accident. It was almost like he was trying to get us out of there, to warn us that we weren't safe. We don't know why Frank chose to stay behind, especially since he didn't die in the mine. His spirit is there by choice. We thought it might have been guilt, or that he wanted to clear his name. Freddy offered another idea: that he didn't understand why he'd survived when two other men died.

In the mine, it took a believer and a skeptic to crack the case. John Tenney believes it should take more than just a haunted village—or the entire paranormal community—to participate in these conversations. "Thinking about these things gives us the opportunity, the motive and the means to talk to each other about our deepest introspective thoughts, our worries, our concerns, our fears," he said. "If that's all ghosts are, a mechanism to talk to each other about our deep emotional experiences, then that's very important. The world needs that. It needs us to talk to each other. If that's what ghosts are doing, if they're giving us weird experiences just so we can talk to each other about weird experiences, that's super important, too. The world is weird."

UNEXPECTED GUESTS IN ST. AUGUSTINE

One of the best things about running paranormal events is that I can return to my favorite haunted spots over and over again. The St. Augustine

Lighthouse, in St. Augustine, Florida, is definitely one of those spots.

Built in 1874, the lighthouse has accumulated a lot of ghosts—but because of the acoustics and the ambient noise, it can be difficult to investigate, especially with a large group of people. Someone can whisper from downstairs and it sounds like it's in your ear. It takes a coordinated effort, and for everyone to be mindful and aware of the noises they're making, to be able to experience much of anything. If you can get it right, though, investigating a lighthouse is so rewarding. They tend to have so much activity, both from the energy people put into them and their position near the ocean, which is believed to give off energy, too.

One night, I was in the basement of the lighthouse, leading a group investigation. It was dark, and there were about fifteen people there. As I looked across the room, I saw some people sitting on a bench: one tall man, and a person on either side of him.

Something immediately felt off. I had been with these same people for a weekend, but I didn't recognize that man. Had he snuck into the group?

I briefly turned my attention the other way, and when I turned back, he was gone.

"Who was that guy sitting between you?" I asked the two.

They said no one had been with them.

Chapter 12

YOU DON'T NEED TO PROVE THAT GHOSTS EXIST

OKAY, MAYBE THIS chapter title sounds odd coming from me—but if you've made it this far and you're having reactions like that, well, that's on you. I promised a lot of weirdness in this book.

The fact of the matter is you're never going to change anyone's mind about the paranormal. You're never going to "prove" to a skeptic that you've had a genuine supernatural experience. You could have the most compelling evidence in the world, and people who are hell-bent on debunking it will find a way to prove (to themselves, at least) that it's fake.

"I never felt the need to prove the paranormal exists to anyone. I simply wanted to understand the phenomena in order to help people cope with it, not try to prove the existence of an afterlife," Grant Wilson said. Since leaving the original *Ghost Hunters*, he's now leading the team on a new version of the show on A&E. "Besides, have you seen what they can do in movies these days? No amount of visual or audio evidence is going to convince anyone of anything in these days of digital trickery."

His view of skeptics is they're just people who have not had supernatural experiences yet. "Why should they be expected to believe without a reason? We should no more expect them to believe than they should expect us to not believe," Grant said. "It's never been about proving to a panel of skeptics the afterlife exists. It's about keeping both feet on the ground while maintaining an open mind. We are exploring avenues that science flat-out rejects, yet accepts when it is convenient for them. We shouldn't expect skeptics to believe without having had an experience that forces them to think differently. And they shouldn't shut down everything we experience without due diligence."

I believe that's true—but I've also encountered skeptics who are so frequently trying to pull me into debates where it's almost like they're daring me to change their minds. The most common objection I get is, "Well, if ghosts are real, why haven't I seen a video of one?" The short answer is: It's hard to get them on video. If you've ever been on an investigation, think about how hard it is to even be sure if you've seen something that's directly in front of your face, and how rarely a ghost will fully appear to you.

The longer answer has to do with camera angles, lighting, and the fact that ghosts just aren't that good at hitting their marks. On *Kindred Spirits*, we work with a limited crew. There are two camera operators, a sound operator, a producer, and a production manager on location with us. That's incredibly small for a show like ours (and has led to a lot of close encounters with the spirit world, which have definitely made some of the behind-the-scenes people believers). Because the show is about me and Adam, and the way we investigate, the cameras are always focused on us and what we're doing. A ghost will appear—in the rare occurrence when one actually *does* appear—for a split second. Barely long enough for us to register its presence. In a lot of instances, only one of us sees it, because it disappears that quickly.

The cameras that film the show are much more sophisticated than simple point-and-shoots, so it takes a few minutes to readjust a shot, especially when the cameraman is doing a close-up and is trying to transition to film something far away. We've experimented with body cams to try to capture what we're seeing, but the footage comes out so bouncy that it would make you seasick to watch it. And while we capture anomalies on the DVR cams quite often, it's nearly impossible to blanket an entire space with them, especially since they work off infrared (IR) light and can compete with each other and cause glare issues.

When we finally make contact with someone who dreamed of being a movie star, maybe we'll be able to ask her to stand in a certain spot while we adjust our cameras to be able to fully capture her image. But until then, we're just going to have to keep working the way we have been. And honestly, even if we did manage to make that happen, someone would *still* say we faked it.

There have been plenty of times when we've captured something that, to me, seems indisputable. You would be shocked at how inventive people can be in coming up with ways that we have "obviously faked" that evidence. Or, if you've looked at social media at any point in the last decade and seen how toxic it can be, maybe you wouldn't be surprised at all. People claim that we fake our EVPs, or that the sounds we capture are our crew making noise off-screen.

I think it's pretty common knowledge that some shows might enhance or play up certain storytelling aspects, but it's fairly easy to figure out which ones they are. Those are purely for entertainment. People love spooky stories, and I am definitely one of them. To me, our show is much different than that. We look for genuine experiences and try our hardest to help people—and as you've probably seen, sometimes that means we come up with almost no evidence, or evidence we weren't looking for, and sometimes it means telling people what they don't want to hear. I wish we could just fake it and come up with answers that would make people happy 100 percent of the time. That's just not the nature of the work we do. And honestly, I'm just not that good an actor. Every time you hear me get bleeped on the show, or see me jump half out of my skin, that's a totally real response.

"I've been part of shows where it's the other side," our former showrunner Brian Garrity said. "Let's just say…you make sure something happens. That's the one thing when working with Adam and Amy that was such a different experience. It's not like somebody talking on the walkie and being like, 'All right, you ready? Here we go.' It's hard to explain without showing too many people's hands as far as how they make TV, but working with them was by far one of the more real experiences I've had working in that genre of television."

A contrarian might say that any television program is inherently entertainment, and that's definitely true. I see our show as purely entertainment for people who don't believe in ghosts. They could very well think it's spooky, but also that I'm faking it the whole time. But *Kindred Spirits* is also for people who *do* believe in ghosts and spirits, who can watch us and know that we do have integrity and empathy. We will never fake anything, and we will always research the history to the best of our ability. It's the real deal. Maintaining our integrity is our first priority on the show. People may imply you're wrong all day long, and poke holes in your research and your evidence, but if you know your truth, it will not affect what you do and how you do it. I always want to be able to look my daughter in the eye and tell her I never once lied in a business wherein people expect you to lie.

As long as you are finding the truth, that's really all that matters. The most bulletproof way you can find that truth is by having solid research, and relying on facts rather than legends. We owe it to ourselves, and to these historic places, to uncover the truth about them. Even if we can't prove ghosts exist in a place, at least we can uncover and ensure factual information for a location.

"There is an increasingly diminishing understanding of and respect for the true goal of the paranormal investigation field," Grant said. "It's not about finding ghosts or proving the afterlife exists. It's about gathering information to truly understand why someone thinks they have a paranormal problem. Eighty percent of the time I can explain paranormal claims through mundane reasons: bad plumbing, sleep deprivation, carbon monoxide poisoning, attention seeking, you name it. It's more about proving the 'normal' exists, rather than proving that the paranormal exists."

In most of the cases when people haven't been happy with our findings, it's because we did not uncover *enough* evidence of the supernatural, or because what we discovered in historical records does not match the stories they've been told and believe to be true. At the Twisted Vine, one of the things we focused on initially was a massive flood that overtook the town in 1955, unearthing coffins in the graveyard. Bodies were floating down the river. It was gruesome. But people in the restaurant had been told that the building had been used as a makeshift morgue, and they thought the activity might be tied to that. When we found that their ghost was totally unrelated to the incident, and had died in 1913, they were surprised, but ultimately just glad to have an explanation.

The people at the Twisted Vine took the news well—that's not an example of someone who has been upset by our findings. But in cases where people have been dismayed with our results, the only thing I've had to rely on is the facts of the situation as I found them through research. Still, like I said, you can't change someone's mind. I really don't think you should even try to. Believing in ghosts is a personal conviction like any other. You shouldn't try to change anyone's mind about their belief system. Either you will believe, or you won't, but you make the choice yourself.

And really, when it comes down to it, who cares if people believe you? To me, that's not the point of paranormal investigation—it's to observe and learn for your own enjoyment. You're reading this book because you're interested in the paranormal. Maybe you'll go on an investigation or to an event one day, and learn more there. It's all about your own personal development. The people who are intent on doubting you aren't going to change their minds until they have an experience of their own.

"I don't see 'believer' and 'skeptic' as mutually exclusive," Grant said. "Many skeptics are simple believers of their own ideas so much so that they reject facts and reality, which is exactly how skeptics themselves view believers." Grant identifies as both. "I have had amazing experiences that no one has been able to explain to me, yet I am skeptical of every experience and all evidence that is presented to me. We should only present something as paranormal if we have exhausted all of our knowledge and the knowledge of those expert professionals who are brave enough to consult with us."

Even after all this, though, I don't think there's a single person in the world who hasn't experienced some kind of strange coincidence, or some kind of odd synchronicity. "Those experiences are the universe giving you messages," John Tenney said in one of his lectures. It can be as simple as a song playing on the radio at the exact right time, or someone calling you just as you were reaching for the phone to call them.

They're not, he believes, just simple coincidences. "When scientists tell you none of this is real, that it's all a coincidence—well, the dictionary definition of that is seemingly unrelated events, which for no discernible reason, are seemingly related. That's a bullshit definition. It means we don't know why they happen. So when a scientist tells you it's just a coincidence, the scientist is literally telling you, 'I have no idea why that happens.' It's not an explanation. It's their way of saying we don't know."

Not knowing, to me, is half the fun—because then we get to find out. Grant continues, "I have had amazing experiences that I can't explain: having to sit and wait for furniture in a living room to stop moving so I can walk past it, being smacked hard in the face by a shadowy form hard enough to spin me around and knock me down. Yet I still scrutinize every experience and piece of evidence that comes my way. If I can't explain it, it's paranormal to me. That doesn't mean it is a ghost, it just means I can't explain it…yet."

THE GHOSTS OF THE OTESAGA HOTEL

Years ago, I was doing an event at the Otesaga Hotel in Cooperstown, New York. It's a notoriously haunted place that is over a century old and was a boarding school for decades.

The fifth floor of the hotel supposedly had a more angry presence up there. We were planning on taking guests there to investigate, so I wanted to do a walk-through with a psychic who was also working at the event to get an idea of the presence and to make sure it wasn't something really negative.

This was more than a decade ago, when I was still learning the basics of hosting group investigations, and this psychic was really big on me trying to use my own intuition as we walked through the space. "Tell me which room you get a vibe on," he said as we walked down the hallway. It was the middle of the day, and there were no guests on the floor because we were going to be using it.

As we were walking past one room, I definitely got a weird feeling. "I feel something here," I said.

When we opened the door, he immediately felt an angry presence. It also had to be 85°F in that room, even though the thermostat wasn't on.

"Is this because he's angry?" I asked.

"Sometimes it can be," he said.

"So what do we do?" I asked.

"Let's just talk to him," the psychic said. "Tell him what's going to happen in here."

So I did. "Tonight there's going to be a lot of people coming in and out of this space, and no one means you any harm," I said. "They all just want to get to know you. They want to know about the history of the hotel. They're just going to be here tonight. I realize that might be upsetting to you, but if there's anything you want to say to them, you should definitely not hesitate to say hello." I talked to him like you would talk to anyone who was reluctant to meet a group of people.

"Does it feel different?" I asked.

"Yeah, I think that worked," he said.

As we were leaving the room, all of a sudden, a piece of molding flew off the doorframe. Not fell, flew. We could hear the *pop, pop, pop* as the nails holding it in place were pulled from the wall. It flew directly, forcefully at me. Straight at me.

Clearly whoever was in that room wasn't interested in making friends.

We locked that room and didn't let anyone in there that night.

Chapter 13

DON'T BELIEVE EVERYTHING YOU READ

IT ONLY KEEPS getting weirder, right? But hear me out on this one, because of all the things I've said in this book, I mean this one the most.

Do not, under any circumstances, take anything you've read in this book as indisputable fact.

When it comes to the supernatural, there is no absolute truth. There is no one, universal knowledge. (Well, there probably is, but we're not going to understand it in this lifetime. See? Stop listening to me.)

All there is, at least on this plane, is one huge conversation. I'm one voice in it. Each person in this book is another single voice. Because of our experience and our public-facing jobs, our voices may be amplified, but that doesn't mean that my ideas are any more "right" than your ideas.

Maybe your experiences create insight that I don't have. (In that case, @ me, because I would love to hear from you.)

"If anyone ever tells you that something is definitively a demon or ghosts, they're leading you down a wrong path, because no one in this field knows what's going on," John Tenney said. "We just know that *something* is going on. I've done this for thirty years, and I'm continually put into experiences that radically shift how I think about the paranormal."

There is magic—at least, an element of the unexplained—all around us every day. On that Strange Escapes at Sea through the Bermuda Triangle, there were garlic ropes strung around the bridge, where the captain controls the ship. "It's to keep away evil spirits," he explained to us on a tour. "When you're on a ship like this, you take every precaution, no matter what it is. We just want to make sure everything is good up here."

As I write this, we're in the middle of a global pandemic, the likes of which our generation has never seen. My state is still under a stay-at-home order to slow the spread of the novel coronavirus, and though people are excitedly talking about opening some states, some feel it's too soon to do so and could result in worsening the situation rather than improving it. It's still far too early to tell what's going to happen, or when this is going to end. None of us—barring those who can actually predict the future—know what the ultimate outcome is going to be.

But I do think I know one thing that will result from the coronavirus: Interest in the paranormal is going to become even stronger than it is now.

Historically, after massive events that change the world as we know it, interest in what's beyond this life has skyrocketed. The American Civil War is directly tied to the rise of the Spiritualism movement, and the popularity of mediums, séances, and spirit photos. Hans Holzer and Ed and Lorraine Warren, in the first wave of paranormal celebrities, became widely known during and just after the Vietnam War. After 9/11, the interest in the paranormal created an environment where *Ghost Hunters*, which started filming in 2003 and premiered in 2004, shot to instant fame as the first paranormal reality TV show. After a major, widespread trauma, people need closure, and they look for answers anywhere they might be able to find them.

Judging by what's happened in the past, I think there's going to be a surge in interest in the paranormal after all of this is over (which, I hope, is when you're reading this book). But more than just read other people's work and look for answers there, I hope you take all those ideas, mash them up in your head, and add your own thoughts. And then, go out and find your own answers, and develop your own theories, too. Every voice is as valid as the next in this conversation about the afterlife. It started long before us, and it will go on long after we're gone.

I've already started seeing this, even during the

pandemic, in the way that more and more people have started noticing and talking about potential paranormal activity in their homes. People are mentioning to me left and right that they're having weird experiences, and for the first time, they think their house might be haunted.

There's definitely something to be said for the increased amount of time we're spending in our homes. We've had a lot of opportunity to observe quirks that we've been too busy or too noisy to notice before. But I also think it might be possible that we're causing this activity to spike because of the pervasive fear and anxiety we are experiencing during the coronavirus crisis. To me, what's happening right now is almost like one massive intention experiment. There are billions of people right now in a perpetual state of anxiety and stress, and all of that energy adds up. People have died alone. People have lost loved ones and not been able to gather with family to say goodbye. The elderly, isolated in nursing homes and care facilities, have not been able to see their families in what could be the last months of their lives. Others, working on the front lines, have gone into work every day knowing they are putting themselves and their families at risk, but they have no choice but to go.

People have lost their livelihoods, struggled to feed their families, lost businesses they sacrificed everything to build. People who suddenly find themselves deemed "essential workers" are still making minimum wage, and without proper protective equipment, so we can have groceries and gas. People are trapped at home in abusive situations, with no way to get out.

Even if you have been lucky enough to be safe, and to be able to stay home with steady employment, you have probably still been struggling with isolation and fear. Compared to many others, my own quarantine has been relatively easy. But explaining to my daughter why she can't go to school or see her friends and that we don't know when it will end—while trying to be strong for her every time I see her little heart break with another piece of bad news—has been one of the hardest things I've ever gone through.

What we have been experiencing is not going to just disappear once we are allowed to freely leave our homes and society opens back up again. The vaccine, if and when we have one for the coronavirus, isn't going to heal our hearts. We are all collectively adding to a worldwide amount of negative energy from all this suffering and struggling— not because we *want* to, but because we are in a very difficult situation and we are feeling how we have every right to feel. I think this might have something to do with the perceived increase of activity in people's homes than there has been in the past. Maybe someone is just discerning it for the first time, or maybe someone else has noisy pipes they never noticed before—or maybe the energy in a home has changed because of how we feel about what we're going through, and that's triggering something to happen.

I don't have any answers. Right now, I'm just trying to keep my family happy and do my part to raise our collective spirits (you know what I mean) when I can. When this is all over, though, I am so curious to see what's going to happen. I think it will change the way we think about the paranormal, and it will definitely affect what happens with my show and my work in general.

But honestly, that's what I love so much about my work. There is always another conversation to have.

"I think people have a hunger for mysterious things," said Aaron Mahnke, creator of the massively popular *Lore* podcast that tells real stories of the unusual and unexplained. "They represent unfinished puzzles, or holes that need to be plugged, and our minds and souls want to fill in the gaps. Whether it's true crime, a thrilling novel, or the world of ghosts and unusual creatures, people have always been drawn to the mystery."

The very first time I saw a ghost, I wanted to know what it was. Decades, and thousands upon thousands of ghost encounters later, my reaction is exactly the same. Delving into the unknown is a passion I will always have—not just because it's interesting to me, not just because I want to solve the case, but because there is always more to know, always a continued conversation to have, always another piece of the mystery to uncover.

Acknowledgments

This book truly took a village. I owe an incredible debt of gratitude to a whole lot of people for making this happen, and I can't tell you how thankful I am to have each and every one of these folks in my life.

Adam Berry—My partner in crime on television, BFF off-screen. I never would have found my way in this paranormal world without you by my side for so much of it. There's good reason I always told Charlotte to call you Uncle Adam. You and I will be like family always. Huge hugs to HusBen, too, xoxo.

Greg and Dana Newkirk—Your friendship and loyalty over these last few years has been incredible. I'm constantly blown away by your ideas and revelations in this field, not to mention your willingness to answer the phone every time we came calling for thoughts on parts of this book. THANK YOU.

John Tenney—Like so many others out there, I never

get tired of hearing what's going on in that mad mind of yours. There's a reason you're so prevalent in this text: Your thoughts and ideas corresponded with or led me to so many revelations in my own beliefs and I thank you for that. You constantly inspire me.

Chip Coffey—You've been my shoulder to cry on more times than I can count. While I value our working relationship, our friendship is one that I treasure more than I can describe here. Thank you so much for your invaluable guidance in my life, and for lending your voice to this work.

Matt, Sarah, and Becky—My wild siblings. We were basically raised by wolves, but look at us now. I love you all more than words can say. Your support over the years as I've navigated this strange and unusual path has meant the world to me.

Steve Gonsalves, Jason Hawes, Dave Tango, Kris Williams, and Grant Wilson—My OG *Ghost Hunters* crew. I'll never forget being welcomed into your unbelievable world in the early days. I know there were rough patches, but what family doesn't have those moments? Each of you has meant so much to me in different ways and you will always be my road family. We've come so far over the years and I love the times I get to reconnect with each and every one of you.

Bill Stankey—Manager extraordinaire, who always makes it happen when I come to him with crazy project ideas. (Like this one!)

Julie Tremaine—Fellow Disney nerd, instant friend, and the only person I could trust with helping me get all these words and ideas into a book.

Grand Central Publishing, especially Gretchen Young—Thanks for appreciating my spooky vision in this and for being such amazing champions as these chapters took shape.

To all the following in the paranormal world who have been so willing to help me over the years: Dave Schrader, Britt Griffith, the Leimkuehler family, Sarah Coombs, Loren Coleman, Aaron Mahnke, Jeff Belanger, Andrea Perron, Aaron Sagers, Karl Pfeiffer, Connor Randall, Auntie Lizzie, Auntie Roxi, and all my friends at Travel Channel and Paper Route Productions. And of course, all the Escapees who come back again and again.

Finally, all of you reading this. Fans, viewers, social media followers—you've all helped me grow over the years and stuck with me on this most magical journey. Thank you.

About the Author

Amy Bruni started working professionally as a paranormal investigator in 2007, when she began appearing on *Ghost Hunters*, one of the longest-running and highest-rated paranormal television shows. Now she's the co-star and executive producer of the Travel Channel's *Kindred Spirits*. In addition, Amy is the owner of Strange Escapes, a company offering guided tours and weekend getaways for paranormal enthusiasts.